22 DAYS IN AUSTRALIA

THE ITINERARY PLANNER
THIRD EDITION

JOHN GOTTBERG

John Muir Publications
Santa Fe, New Mexico

In Fond Memory of the Blue Minx

This book would not have been possible without the assistance of the Australian Tourist Commission, the various state and territory tourist commissions, and the following individuals: Linda Carlock, Rick Steves, Cesare Cataldo, Peggy Bendel, Elaine Kleckner, Patrick J. O'Reilly, Gina Dodd, John Greenslade, Sue Brennan, Sara Longwood, Don Knapp, Amanda Struthers, Scott Thornton, Bob Schatz, Julie and Kevin Keir, Deb and Greg Derwin, Linda and Alan Mulley, Margaret and John Bee.

Suggestions from Dolores Atallo, Leanne Davis, Michelle Goggin, Marty Kane, Laurie Martin and Cait Falck have been incorporated in this third edition.

John Muir Publications, P.O. Box 613, Santa Fe, NM 87504

Third edition. First printing

Library of Congress Cataloging-in-Publication Data
Gottberg, John.
    22 days in Australia : the itinerary planner/John Gottberg.
  — 3rd ed.
    p.   cm.
    ISBN 0-945465-40-8
    1. Australia—Description and travel—1981- —Guide-books.
I. Title.   II. Title: Twenty-two days in Australia.
DV95.404'63—dc20   89-42951
                                            CIP

Distributed to the book trade by:
W.W. Norton & Company, Inc.
New York, New York

Design   Mary Shapiro
Maps   Jim Wood
Cover Map   Michael Taylor
Typography   Copygraphics, Inc.

CONTENTS

Australia in 22 Days

G'day! In your hands is your fair dinkum, pocket-sized Aussie tour guide. It's designed for independent-minded blokes and birds who like the freedom and flexibility of going walkabout their own way but who appreciate the efficiency that an organized tour offers.

22 Days in Australia doesn't pretend to take you around the entire continent of "Oz" in three weeks. That would be like trying to see the whole United States in 22 days. It's a fair comparison: Australia is almost identical in size to the 48 contiguous states.

What I have tried to do in this itinerary is to provide a sampling of Australia's most fascinating features—from the great cities of Sydney and Melbourne, to predictable (and worthwhile!) tourist stops such as the Great Barrier Reef and Ayers Rock, to less-known sites like reconstructed gold rush towns and an island of nesting penguins—and suggest how to appreciate them most thoroughly while getting the maximum value for your travel dollar.

Because Australia is so vast, in order to see as much as possible within a three-week itinerary, you should rely on domestic airlines to cover large chunks of land between major attractions. Most of Australia's 16 million people live along the relatively fertile southeast coast, an area well equipped with good roads and visitor facilities. The same is not true of the outback. To get to the dry Centre from any direction, you are faced with a journey of many hundreds of miles across bleak, foreboding terrain. It is probably not a good idea to drive yourself there. Air travel, while no bargain, can save considerable time and worry. With extra time, much of the trip can be done by rental car or (more cheaply and reliably but with somewhat less freedom) by train and bus.

The trip outlined in this book begins in Sydney and concludes in Brisbane. International flights also serve Melbourne and Cairns, allowing you to start and end in any of these gateway cities. I suggest that you take an extra Friday off work and leave home on Thursday night, arriving in Sydney on Saturday morning to begin your adventure. This will make connections easier later in the trip (especially on the sporadic Alice Springs-Cairns air leg) and will allow you a full day to recover from jet lag at home before going back to work when your vacation's finished.

I like to compare any travel plan to a childhood Erector set. The itinerary should provide a framework for travel but should not restrict the wanderer from indulging personal interests or whims. Take this itinerary and customize it to your own needs and wants. Make changes. Scribble in the margins. Cross things out; add new ones. Spend extra time in one place if it intrigues you, skip another if you find it boring. If there are things you'd like to do in Australia which I haven't listed in this book—by all means, do them.

Each chapter is modular in itself and can be included as part of whatever itinerary you may want to develop. The 22 days are organized around the same features (though not always in this order):

1. An **Introductory Overview** of the day.
2. An hour-by-hour **Suggested Schedule** for the day.
3. A list of **Sightseeing Highlights** (rated: ▲▲▲ Don't miss; ▲▲ Try hard to see; ▲ Worthwhile if you can make it).
4. **Orientation** and an easy-to-read map of the area.
5. **Transportation** tips and instructions.
6. **Accommodations and Dining:** How and where to find the best places in your price range, including addresses, phone numbers, and my favorites.
7. **Itinerary options** for those travelers with more or less than the suggested time or with particular interests.

At the back of the book, I've included some optional tour extensions, which expand on the main itinerary.

In deciding when and where to launch your trip, consider holiday and event schedules and seasonal weather trends. January through March are the rainiest months along the northern Barrier Reef, for example, while June to September give the Snowy Mountains their name. Spring (October to mid-December) and autumn (mid-March to May) are the best months to cover all corners of this schedule.

Paperwork
To travel to Australia, you will need a valid passport and a tourist visa. Your tourist visa will cost you nothing except the price of a passport-sized photograph and a self-addressed stamped (and registered) envelope. Your travel agent can handle everything for you. Allow a couple of weeks for processing. A tourist visa to Australia is typically good for up to six months, with multiple entries allowed for five years or the life of the passport. The tourist visa does prohibit you from working, seeking employment, or taking a major course of study while you are in Australia. These require separate visas that must be obtained from outside the country.

Australian consular offices in the United States are located at:

1601 Massachusetts Ave., N.W., Washington, D.C. 20036 (tel. 202/797-3000)

636 5th Ave., New York, NY 10111 (tel. 212/245-4000)

Suite 2930, Quaker Tower, 321 N. Clark St., Chicago, IL 60610 (tel. 312/645-9444)

1990 Post Oak Blvd., Suite 800, Houston, TX 77056 (tel. 713/629-9131)

611 N. Larchmont Blvd., Los Angeles, CA 90046 (tel. 213/469-4300)

360 Post St., San Francisco, CA 94108 (tel. 415/362-6160)

1000 Bishop St., Honolulu, HI 96813 (tel. 808/524-5050)

Offices in Canada are located at:

Suite 710, 50 O'Connor St., Ottawa, Ontario K1P 6L2 (tel. 613/236-0841)

Suite 2200 Commerce Court West, King and Bay Streets, Toronto, Ontario M5L 189 (tel. 416/367-0783)

1066 W. Hastings St., Vancouver, B.C. V6E 3X1 (tel. 604/684-1177)

Cost Considerations

Prices in Australian dollars for transportation, accommodation, food, and so forth, are roughly what you might expect to pay in the United States. The good news is that the Australian dollar is worth about 78.5 U.S. cents at this writing (August 1989), which means that when you're paying A$30 for a hotel room, you're actually only paying US$23.50. The same goes for restaurants, where you can pay A$10 for an excellent four-course dinner: in U.S. dollars, you're actually only paying around $7.85.

The prices estimated and quoted in this book are based on two people traveling together and sharing hotel rooms. If you're traveling alone, you can expect to spend somewhat more. If you're traveling with a larger group, it will cost you a bit less, especially when it comes to hotel rooms and taxi fares. The cost of meals and public transportation won't change much.

Excluding costs of airfares to and from Australia—about US$1,000 to US$1,500 from the U.S. West Coast—budget travelers can do this 22-day trip for around US$1,500. The budget traveler will stay in hostel-style lodging for A$15 a night or less, travel by bus or train between Sydney and Melbourne, and spend A$880 to fly the Melbourne-Alice Springs-Cairns-Brisbane legs of the trip. If it's not important to keep to the 22-day itinerary limit, you can shell out A$500 for a 21-day bus pass in lieu of the airfares—although your additional outlay for meals and accommodations will minimize the actual savings.

This trip is ideally suited and designed for the traveler with a little more money in his or her pocket—say, US$2,500 for the three-week journey, not including getting there. If you are this middle-ground tourist, you'll spend an average of A$30 a night for a shared hotel room with private facilities, rent a car for the Sydney-Canberra-Melbourne highway leg, purchase an air pass, and book the occasional tour, like a cruise to the outer Barrier Reef.

The traveler who likes to go everywhere in style, to stay at the best hotels and eat at the best restaurants, will also find this itinerary appropriate. You can do this within a budget of US$3,500 per person, splitting the cost of A$100-a-night hotel rooms, renting a car wherever you want, traveling on an air pass, and booking numerous side tours and cruises during your visit.

The Australian dollar, by the way, is hard to find in paper these days. It's been replaced in everyday use by a A$1 gold-colored coin, leaping kangaroos on the flip side of Queen Elizabeth's portrait. Other coins are the heavy, 12-sided 50-cent piece, the 20-cent piece (slightly larger than an American quarter), the 10-cent piece (similar in size to a dime), the 5-cent piece (about like a Canadian 5-center), the 2-cent piece (copper, bigger than a penny) and the 1-cent penny (much like ours). Paper money, from the lime-green A$2 note to the blue-gray A$100, grows in size and changes color as denominations increase. (In between are $5, $10, $20, and $50 notes.)

It is safest to carry your U.S. dollars in the form of traveler's checks, which you can exchange at city banks 9:30 a.m. to 4:00 p.m. Monday to Thursday and 9:30 a.m. to 5:00 p.m. Friday and at airport currency counters or major hotel desks anytime.

When to Go

Australia's big tourist season is during the school holidays, which fall in the middle of summer, appropriately—December, January, and into February. This is the warmest time of year Down Under, but for four very good reasons, this is NOT a time of year when I would recommend going to Australia:

(1) This is when the Australians are on holiday. You'll find most attractions as well as accommodations heavily booked, and there's a lot of competition to get hold of rental cars, which tends to drive prices up a bit.

(2) This is the rainy season in north Queensland; indeed, it's sometimes the cyclone season. Torrents of rain fall in the northern Barrier Reef (Cairns-Townsville) area, especially from January to March. Don't go without your brolly (umbrella).

(3) Blowflies—some call them the Australian national bird—are vicious anytime in the outback, but especially under the hot summer sun.

(4) Perhaps most of all, December through March are classified as "high season" by international airlines, which jack up their fares 35 to 50 percent during this period. You can add US$200 to US$400 to your round-trip airfare if you insist on traveling at this time.

June, July, and August—the North American summer but the Australian winter—are superb in the tropics and subtropics, but the farther south you go, the less pleasant you're likely to find the weather. Melbourne, for example, whose climate is comparable to San Francisco, can easily have four seasons in a day. What's more, as you travel through Canberra into the Snowy Mountains, you're almost guaranteed to run into snow, and that may cause the closure of some roads.

In my estimation, the ideal times for travel in Australia are autumn (mid-March through May) and spring (September to November). On average, the climate is the best at that time in all parts of the country, and you won't be fighting for rooms like you might be during the peak summer season.

What to Bring
As little as possible. Traveling light frees you from the trials of vagabondage to enjoy your journey more thoroughly. Unless you're in Oz in the winter or are prone to straying into higher elevations, you shouldn't need anything warmer than a sweater and possibly a rain jacket. Cairns, in far north Queensland, is at the same latitude south as Guatemala is north, and it's equally as tropical. The southernmost point on the Australian continent, near Melbourne, if flipped across the Equator, would be no farther north than Washington, D.C., or Lake Tahoe.

Tend toward lighter clothes, wash-and-wear items that you can wash in your hotel room and dry overnight. I take what I wear and two more sets of everything. Some say I overpack. Australia is a very informal country, and unless you plan to do business on Collins Street in Melbourne (the only city in Australia where a coat and tie are almost prerequisite), you'll be fine in any situation with a long-sleeved shirt and slacks or a plain top and wraparound skirt.

If you're going to use them, bring a camera and lenses (as few as necessary). Buy your film in Australia. You'll want sunglasses for the beaches and the desert; if you get to the outback and discover you need a wide-brimmed hat with character, choose one there. A good pair of walking shoes is essential. Of course, one thing you should never travel without is a sense of humor.

Flying to Australia

The cheapest fares from North America are from the West Coast gateway cities of Los Angeles, San Francisco, and Vancouver (Canada). It is occasionally possible to find cut-rate or charter tickets for as little as US$800 round-trip. During the April-through-November "low season," you should plan on spending US$950, perhaps up to US$1,100, for an APEX (advance purchase excursion) fare. In December, Australia's "high season," a round-trip APEX fare can run up to US$1,500. October-November and January-February are the "shoulder season," with in-between fares.

Trans-Pacific flights leave the West Coast between 8:00 and 11:00 p.m., arriving in Sydney a day and a half later (after crossing the International Date Line) sometime between 6:00 and 9:00 a.m. Qantas, the Australian national flag carrier, flies daily from both San Francisco and Los Angeles, often with stopovers in Honolulu or Tahiti. Nightly service is also offered by Air New Zealand from Los Angeles to Auckland and Sydney via Tahiti or Honolulu and/or Fiji; by United Airlines from Los Angeles to Sydney, nonstop or via Honolulu; and by Continental Airlines from San Francisco and Los Angeles. Canadian Pacific Airlines flies twice weekly from Vancouver to Sydney via Honolulu and/or Fiji, while UTA French Airlines has weekly services from Los Angeles to Sydney via Tahiti, Auckland, and Noumea, New Caledonia.

Flights originating from the U.S. East Coast are routed through either of the California cities. It's also possible to connect in Great Britain or Europe with Australia-bound flights of Qantas, British Airways, Lufthansa, KLM Dutch Airlines, Air India, Cathay Pacific, Singapore Airlines, and others.

Sydney is 18 hours ahead of the U.S. West Coast, 15 hours ahead of New York and the East Coast. When you travel west across the Pacific, you're crossing the International Date Line, so you lose a day. Not to worry, the Aussies would say. She'll be right. You'll pick up that day coming home again.

Of course, if you keep moving west, you won't pick up that day. That's something to consider: for US$2,500, roughly twice the amount of your round-trip ticket, you could fly around the world. For US$2,000, you could invest in a circle-Pacific fare and take in Asia. Read more about those options in *Asia Through the Back Door* (Santa Fe, N.M.: John Muir Publications, 1990), by Rick Steves and me.

Getting Around in Australia

As I mentioned earlier, within the context of this three-week itinerary, it is most efficient to fly across large chunks of otherwise tedious territory. The cost-wise way to do this is through discount airfares.

Ansett Airlines' "See Australia" plan knocks 25 percent off standard coach fares for 1,000 or more kilometers of air travel within the country. Anyone who travels round-trip to Australia on an APEX or similar excursion ticket is eligible. Make arrangements (and flight reservations) through your travel agent before you leave home or at an Ansett office within 30 days of your arrival in Australia.

The flight segments recommended in this itinerary—Melbourne-Alice Springs-Ayers Rock and Alice Springs-Cairns-Brisbane, some 5,100 km—cost A$881 (US$692) in mid-1989. That's a savings of US$231 over daily airfares.

It's unfortunate that Ansett discontinued its "Go Australia Airpass" in 1988. Until then, one could travel up to 6,000 km for A$600 (US$471), or 10,000 km for A$950 (US$746). One can only hope the airline will reconsider.

Ansett is one of two major domestic carriers in Australia. The other, Australian Airlines, is every bit as good. For our purposes, though, there's one significant difference: Ansett has the sole concession on Alice Springs-to-Ayers Rock air travel. Australian Airlines has a routing edge only in flights to outback Queensland.

Two other transportation pass options may interest budget travelers—bus and train. Three separate motor coach firms with extensive national routes offer passes for unlimited travel within their city-to-city express systems. Deluxe Coachlines, the "Avis" ("we try harder") of the three, has a "Koalapass" valid for 10 to 90 days. (A 14-day pass is A$345, a 21-day pass A$500, a 60-day pass A$955.) Greyhound has an "Australia Bus Pass" that is valid for 15 (A$330) to 60 (A$880) days. Greyhound advertises free city sightseeing in some cities, discount tours in others, for passholders. Discount motel packages are also available in concert with the coach passes.

Railways of Australia have an "Austrailpass" valid for unlimited first-class travel and a "Budget Austrailpass" for unlimited economy travel on its route system. (This system is limited: the only way to travel from Alice Springs to Cairns is on a bus or via Sydney.) The minimum duration is 14 days (A$670 first-class, A$410 budget); one month is A$640 budget, three months cost A$1,030 budget. There's an additional charge for overnight berths (for example, A$28 Brisbane-Cairns; A$47 Adelaide-Alice Springs; A$139 Melbourne-Perth).

My major objection to travel by train or bus is that they carry you only from urban area to urban area. You don't see rural Australia except through smoked windows. Buses and trains pass through an area only two or three times daily; if you want to disembark and take a closer look at something interesting, you're going to have a long wait before the next coach shoots through. You wouldn't even get to the exquisite Victorian gold town of Beechworth; the main-line buses don't go there. And how could you possibly do a wine-tasting tour of Australia's great vineyard districts by bus or train?

Renting a Car and Driving

The best way to see southeastern Australia is to drive your own vehicle. A car allows you much more freedom in your travels, plus an opportunity to get in touch with the "real" Australia. Part of this 22-day tour is geared for the car traveler. If two of you, or better yet, four are traveling together, you'll share the costs of the vehicle and really cut your expenses.

To rent a car in Australia, you must be over 21 years old, preferably have a major credit card, and definitely have a valid driver's license. It is not necessary for you to have an international driver's license. A valid license from any state or Canadian province is quite sufficient.

All major airports have a handful of rental agencies; many are also located in central city areas near major hotels. In Sydney, check the rental agencies on William Street between downtown and Kings Cross. While Hertz and Avis are the old standbys, you'll probably get a better rate from Thrifty or from any number of smaller, locally owned firms.

Plan on an outlay of A$55 to A$65 a day (about US$43 to US$51), including limited kilometers. Petrol (gas), in New South Wales and Victoria priced at 50 to 55 Australian cents a liter (US$1.33 to US$1.46 a gallon), will be your only other major driving expense. (The cost of petrol is slightly cheaper in South Australia and southeastern Queensland, a bit higher in Tasmania and Western Australia.)

Remember that Australia, like most nations of the world, employs the metric system of measurement. There are roughly 3.8 liters to 1 U.S. gallon. Eight kilometers equal about 5 miles.

Your major adjustment driving in Australia rather than North America is that you will be driving a right-hand drive car on the left-hand side of the road. This is not as difficult as you might at first imagine. Everything is simply reversed. Just remember to keep the center line next to the steering wheel, just as you would back home. (But in Australia it's on your right, not on your left.) Your major difficulty may be in turning. Be sure to stay in the left-hand lane: avoid turning across traffic to the right side of the road.

In the cities, you don't need a car and shouldn't use one. It's not worth the frustration, between rush-hour traffic, parking hassles, and confusing local laws. (Downtown Melbourne, for instance, requires drivers to pull all the way to the left of an intersection and wait for traffic to clear before turning right.) Inner city public transportation is very good. Buses, Sydney subways, and Melbourne trams are all excellent. Taxis are moderately priced. Turn your car in on arrival in a new city and save yourself many headaches.

"Petrol" isn't the only new word you'll have to learn for driving Down Under. Your car does not have a trunk and a hood; it has a boot and a bonnet. The windshield is known as the windscreen. You don't pass other vehicles; you overtake them. Roads aren't paved; they're sealed, or covered with bitumen. In cities, pavement is what you find across the kerb (curb) on the footpath (sidewalk).

The only roads in Australia that are really in good condition are the main highways—particularly the Sydney-to-Melbourne Hume Highway, a four-lane thoroughfare. Many other roads are in less than optimum shape, sealed but with no shoulders and with lots of ruts and potholes.

Those signs warning "Next 10 km" of kangaroos or other Aussie animals should be more than curiosities, especially to night drivers. You won't often see wild animals in the daytime, but please drive carefully after dark.

Where to Stay

Australia has a real choice here, with accommodations of all standards at all price levels. I rate budget accommodations as those costing A$20 and less a night; economy, A$20 to A$50; moderate, A$50 to A$100; and deluxe, over A$100. There are a number of categories to consider.

Hotels run the full gamut from the internationally ranked Regent of Sydney all the way down to the corner pub with a few basic rooms in the attic. Deluxe to economy.

Private hotels are not licensed to sell liquor and therefore are usually lower in cost. Moderate and economy. Guest houses are private hotels that provide bed and breakfast, often (but not always) included in the tariff. Moderate and economy.

Self-catering apartments are, in essence, hotel suites with their own cooking facilities and sometimes private laundry facilities. Deluxe and moderate.

Motels in Australia offer much the same as their American counterparts. Deluxe to economy.

Hostels may or may not be members of the International Youth Hostel Federation. IYH member hostels are located in cities, towns, and national parks throughout the country. Private "backpackers hostels" with similar price structures are more recent developments in major cities and tourist centers. Budget.

Caravan parks are not only for caravans (what Americans call "trailers"). You can set up a tent or, in many cases, stay in a small housekeeping cabin with a hotplate. Budget.

Farm holidays will place you on a "station" far from the bright city lights, where you can watch the dogs muster the sheep—or help a jackeroo round up his cattle by helicopter. Write: 9 Fletcher St., Woollahra, Sydney, NSW 2025, for details. Moderate and economy.

What and Where to Eat and Drink

Australia is a very cosmopolitan country. This is especially true in Sydney and Melbourne, which have very large populations of south Europeans, Lebanese, and Asians. Nowhere is their influence felt more strongly than in the variety and quality of reasonably priced cuisine. You can eat well at any meal for under A$12. If you plan to spend A$25 per day per person on food, you're perhaps being a little bit extravagant—or else you're budgeting for an occasional splurge at a classier restaurant.

Though not widely acknowledged, there is an Australian cuisine somewhat more imaginative than the bland British and Irish cooking from which it derived. Aussie "tucker" comprises the like of occasionally palatable dishes such as kangaroo tail soup, meat pies, "snags" (large sausages), damper (unleavened campfire bread), and Vegemite (a strong-tasting yeast spread) and more delectable delicacies such as carpetbagger steak (tenderloin stuffed with Sydney rock oysters), roast lamb in mint sauce, pavlova (a meringue dessert), and superb seafood—yabbies (a small lobster), Moreton Bay bugs (another small crustacean), Tasmanian scallops, and indigenous fish like barramundi, jewfish, and John Dory.

I will typically begin my day in Australia with a light breakfast of fresh fruit—pawpaws (papayas) and mangoes are always in season—and/or pastry with a cup of tea or coffee. Later in the morning I might stop for Devonshire tea, served with fresh scones (with whipped cream and strawberry jam). For lunch, I might pick up some fish and chips or a chicko roll at the takeaway counter of a milk bar (sort of like a 7-11 with a fast-food counter). More often, I'll pause for pub grub. You never really go wrong if you eat in a pub. The price is right—often A$5 to A$8 for a full meal—and you can pick some pretty good meals off the blackboard menu: roast chicken, grilled fish, steak-and-kidney pie, even cook your own T-bone. At dinnertime, I'll often head off to the European or Asian section of town, read the menus posted in the windows, and wander in where I see the locals eating. And I almost always wash it down with a glass of good Aussie beer or wine. Many restaurants acclaim themselves as "BYO": bring your own alcoholic beverage. They may charge a small corkage fee, but their prices are almost always lower than licensed restaurants, and it's no great inconvenience to stop by the bottle shop at a nearby pub (pub = "public hotel").

Beer is the Australian national drink, and it certainly deserves that distinction. Those who compile such statistics say the Aussies drink more beer per capita—some 30 gallons annually—than anyone but the Bavarians and Belgians. Every state has its own breweries and is stubbornly proud of its local brews. Drink from middies or pots (10-ounce glasses) or from schooners (15 ounces).

Australian wine has become recognized as among the best in the world. The principal growing areas are the Barossa Valley, focused on Tanunda northeast of Adelaide, and the Hunter Valley, around Cessnock north of Sydney. Victoria and Western Australia also have excellent wineries. Riesling, semillon, chardonnay, and white burgundy are among the better white wines; in the reds, consider claret, cabernet sauvignon, shiraz, and merlot.

Information Sources

This slender tome is not intended to be more than a travel planner used in conjunction with a more complete guidebook. Lonely Planet's *Australia: A Travel Survival Kit*, by Tony Wheeler et al., has long been the bible of shoestring travelers in Australia, and deservedly so. The book has grown to become a very comprehensive volume of some 400 pages thoroughly covering the entire continent. It is a book that no traveler, especially no budget traveler, should go without. An option, not as detailed nationwide but reasonably good in the major cities, is Frommer's *Australia on $25 a Day* by John Godwin. For middle- and upper-income travelers looking to get the most quality for their dollar, I highly recommend Robert W. Bone's *Maverick Guide to Australia* (Gretna, La.: Pelican). An excellent book for planning your trip and to keep as a souvenir when your trip is over is Apa Publications' lavishly illustrated *Insight Guide: Australia*. You should be able to find any of these books at major bookshops across North America.

In planning, don't overlook the assistance you can get from the Australian Tourist Commission and from the individual state and territory tourist boards. They can provide an enormous amount of valuable information for your journey. They also can provide the best highway maps I've found on Australia and its

separate states. It's all free, and all commissions have offices in
North America:

Australian Tourist Commission
489 Fifth Ave., New York, NY 10017 (tel. 212/687-6300)
3550 Wilshire Blvd., Suite 1740, Los Angeles, CA 90010 (tel.
213/380-6060)
120 Eglinton Ave. E., Suite 220, Toronto, Ontario, Canada M4P
1E2 (tel. 416/487-2126)

New South Wales Tourist Commission
2049 Century Park East, Suite 2250, Los Angeles, CA 90067
(tel. 213/552-9566)

Northern Territory Tourism Commission
3550 Wilshire Blvd., Suite 1610, Los Angeles, CA 90010 (tel.
213/383-7092)

Queensland Tourist and Travel Corporation
489 Fifth Ave., 31st Floor, New York, NY 10017 (tel. 687-6300)
3550 Wilshire Blvd., Suite 1738, Los Angeles, CA 90010 (tel.
213/381-3062)
890 W. Pender St., Suite 600, Vancouver, B.C., Canada V6C
1J9 (tel. 604/687-7975)

South Australian Department of Tourism
2121 Avenue of the Stars, Los Angeles, CA 90067 (tel.
213/552-2821)

Tasmanian Department of Tourism
3550 Wilshire Blvd., Suite 1740, Los Angeles, CA 90010 (tel.
213/380-6060)

Victorian Tourism Commission
3550 Wilshire Blvd., Suite 1736, Los Angeles, CA 90010 (tel.
213/387-3111)

Western Australian Tourism Commission
2121 Avenue of the Stars, Los Angeles, CA 90067 (tel.
213/557-1987)

Other Reading
Nearly all Aussies identify with the outback, the "bush," even if
they are (as are most) urban dwellers. To get a feeling for this tra-
dition, I would go back to the short stories and poetry of
nineteenth-century writers Henry Lawson and A. B. "Banjo"
Paterson. Lawson is more highly acclaimed in Australia, though
Paterson's ballads—"Waltzing Matilda," "The Man from Snowy
River"—are better known to Americans.

The best Australian novel in recent years is Colleen McCul-
lough's *The Thorn Birds*. Some North Americans know the
miniseries (starring Richard Chamberlain) better than the book.
A young Aussie writer who impresses me is Tim Winton (*That
Eye, the Sky*).

Good histories are Donald Horne's *The Australian People: Biography of a Nation* and F. R. Crowley's *A New History of Australia*. Robert Hughes's superb *The Fatal Shore* (1987) deals with Australia's convict history and, indirectly, its impact on the modern nation. For a better understanding of aboriginal history and culture, see *Australian Dreaming*, edited by Jennifer Isaacs. Titles by Michael Morcombe and Eric Worrell are among the best dealing with Australia's rich natural history.

Write Me a Letter
Change affects Australia as it does everywhere in the world. No matter how hard I try to keep this book up to date, there's always going to be something I miss. If this volume helps you enjoy your trip, if it doesn't help you, if you've found things that need more explanation, if you've found things that would add to the enjoyment of other travelers, I would love to hear from you. Please send your tips and recommendations, love mail and hate mail, criticism and corrections, c/o John Muir Publications, P.O. Box 613, Santa Fe, NM 87504. In return for ideas used, I'll send you a free copy of my next edition.

Meanwhile—happy travels!

ITINERARY

Whenever I mention to an Australian that I'm the author of a book entitled *22 Days in Australia*, I'm greeted first with a dazed look, then a chuckle. "Oh, you'd be buggered after that one, mate!" they say as they shout another beer. But the fact remains that most Americans have only, if they're lucky, three weeks of vacation in which to see Australia. So here is my suggested itinerary, which I hope provides the best sampling of the country in a limited period of time. I encourage you to add days for relaxation whenever possible, because the pace of travel—over 4,000 miles in a very short time—can be exhausting. Here is an overview of the 22-day itinerary.

DAY 1 (Saturday) Arrive in Sydney in the morning, get set up in your accommodation, then enjoy an afternoon cruise on beautiful Sydney Harbour. Call it quits right after dinner tonight, cheating jet lag with an early bedtime.

DAY 2 (Sunday) The Sydney Explorer bus will escort you to all major city sights for one set fare. Highlights will include the famous Opera House; the Australian Museum; and The Rocks, Sydney's oldest neighborhood. Enjoy an atmospheric dinner at the Argyle Tavern in The Rocks, with bush ballad sing-alongs.

DAY 3 (Monday) Exercise your options. I like to start the day at Bondi Beach, then visit the colonial Vaucluse House mansion and wander through the suburbs of Double Bay and Paddington. If it's marsupials you want to see, take the ferry across the harbor to Taronga Park Zoo, and include a visit to Manly, with its famous surf beach and Marineland. History buffs may want to visit Old Sydney Town in Gosford; oenophiles should make a side trip to the Hunter Valley. Spend the night at Kings Cross, where you can play or gape at others playing.

DAY 4 (Tuesday) Pick up your reserved rental car in Sydney early this morning, with plans to leave it in Melbourne in a week. After a stop to see the working sheep farm at Gledswood homestead, continue to historic Berrima for lunch. On arrival in Canberra, visit the Regatta Point Planning Exhibition to understand the design and evolution of this modern capital, then drive to the top of Mount Ainslie for a good overview.

DAY 5 (Wednesday) Explore Canberra. Start at the Parliament House, if possible watching the House of Representatives or

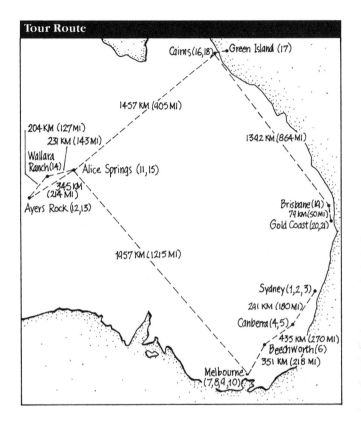

Tour Route

Cairns (16,18) •Green Island (17)

1457 KM (905 MI)

204 KM (127 MI)
231 KM (143 MI)

1342 KM (864 MI)

Wallara
Ranch (14) Alice Springs (11,15)

345 KM
(214 MI)

Ayers Rock (12,13)

Brisbane (19)
79 KM (50 MI)
Gold Coast (20,21)

1957 KM (1215 MI)

Sydney (1,2,3)
291 KM (180 MI)
Canberra (4,5)

435 KM (270 MI)
Beechworth (6)
351 KM (218 MI)

Melbourne
(7,8,9,10)

Senate in session from a public gallery. Take a drive through the
Yarralumla area to see the impressive row of national embassies,
then lunch at the High Court, inspect the National Gallery, and
visit the Australian War Memorial museum.

DAY 6 (Thursday) There's a long day of driving ahead, so get an
early start. Today's route leads past the alpine resort of Thredbo
in the Snowy Mountains and via Corryong, reputed home of
poet Banjo Paterson's "Man from Snowy River," to Beechworth,
a town straight out of the nineteenth-century gold rush era.

DAY 7 (Friday) After a morning look at Beechworth, visit the
Brown Brothers Winery, one of Australia's finest, and stop in
Glenrowan, where Ned Kelly, Australia's most notorious frontier
bushranger, made his "last stand." The afternoon's highlight is
the Sir Colin McKenzie Wildlife Sanctuary at Healesville, an

open-air reserve that is the best of its kind in the world. You'll reach Melbourne in time for dinner.

DAY 8 (Saturday) Explore Melbourne today. Wander through its ethnic neighborhoods, its sophisticated shopping arcades, its highbrow business district. Don't miss the beautiful Victorian Arts Centre or the nation's best botanic gardens. The Old Gaol and the National Museum are worthy stops. But don't overdo the sightseeing. Here in sports-crazy Melbourne, you should soak up some Australian culture with (depending on the season) a visit to a "footie" match, a cricket test, or a horse race.

DAY 9 (Sunday) Drive to Ballarat, site of Australia's greatest gold rush and its most famous rebellion. The Sovereign Hill theme park realistically re-creates the town's heyday. The adjacent Gold Museum and the Eureka Exhibition memorialize Eureka Stockade, the nation's 1854 reply to Bunker Hill. Return to Melbourne in the late afternoon.

DAY 10 (Monday) Drive east into the Dandenong Ranges, where you can wonder at William Ricketts' unique forest sculptures or search for lyrebirds in Sherbrooke Forest. Proceed to Phillip Island, where fairy penguins parade from the sea at dusk. Then return to Melbourne.

DAY 11 (Tuesday) Drop your car at Melbourne's Tullamarine airport and catch a morning flight to Alice Springs. You'll have all afternoon and evening to explore this outback oasis. Stop by the Old Telegraph Station, the Royal Flying Doctor Service, and the Aboriginal art galleries. Climax your day with something unique: ride a camel down the dry Todd River bed to dinner at a desert winery.

DAY 12 (Wednesday) Marvel at the weird geology of the Red Centre as you fly from Alice Springs to Yulara resort village at Ayers Rock, arriving in the early afternoon. After getting settled in your lodging and exploring the community, join the sunset barbecue tour to The Olgas.

DAY 13 (Thursday) Learn about the Aboriginal culture today. Spend the morning with a native guide who will show you how his people found food, water, shelter, and medicine in this arid landscape. Visit the craft exhibit at the Uluru National Park ranger station and search for ancient petroglyphs in caves around the base of Ayers Rock. Back at Yulara, sip champagne as you watch the sun set over the red rock. Turn in early, because tomorrow, if you're energetic, you will . . .

DAY 14 (Friday). . . climb The Rock. If the the world's largest monolith is awesome at sunset, it's even more stunning at dawn. Awaken early to watch the light change its appearance and to beat the heat and flies as you scale the huge red rock so that you, too, can wear a T-shirt declaring, "I Climbed Ayers Rock." Then board a bus for the 125-mile drive to the Wallara Ranch, where you'll spend the night at an outback station.

DAY 15 (Saturday) Scramble through the sheer walls of colorful Kings Canyon, then return to Alice Springs in the evening. If you're not exhausted, enjoy a nightcap at the casino.

DAY 16 (Sunday) A travel day, Alice Springs to Cairns. On arrival in Cairns, the humidity will tell you immediately that you are in the tropics. Have a cold beer at an Esplanade pub and watch the fishing and pleasure boats come and go to the Great Barrier Reef. For dinner, order barramundi, a delectable river-run reef cod.

DAY 17 (Monday) Ship out for Green Island, a tiny coral enclave 40 minutes' cruise offshore where you can swim, study the sea life from a glass-bottom boat, view the largest crocodile in captivity in the world, and dine, drink, and sleep at the small resort.

DAY 18 (Tuesday) You'll leave Green Island this morning to spend the day snorkeling or diving on the outer Barrier Reef. This experience should not be missed. More than 200 species of tropical reef fish can be seen swimming through a fantastic undersea "garden" of multicolored coral. Return to Cairns at night.

DAY 19 (Wednesday) The scenic Kuranda Railway will take you inland to the edge of the rain-forested Atherton Tableland, climbing steeply above fields of sugarcane to the Barron River Gorge. In Kuranda, you'll have time to see Barron Falls, the open-air market, and the Noctarium before returning to Cairns after lunch. Take a late afternoon flight to Brisbane.

DAY 20 (Thursday) Brisbane's No. 1 tourist sight is the Lone Pine Koala Sanctuary, Australia's largest. If you ever wanted a photo of yourself holding one of these seemingly cuddly creatures, here's where to have it taken. Travel there by boat up the

Brisbane River. After lunch, take a bus to the Gold Coast, Australia's version of Miami Beach. Catch the day's last rays on the beach.

DAY 21 (Friday) Your final day on Australian beaches. The Gold Coast's biggest town is called Surfers Paradise; why not decide for yourself if the name really fits? Or you can dive into tourist attractions such as Sea World, the Currumbin Bird Sanctuary, or the Mudgeeraba Boomerang Factory.

DAY 22 (Saturday) It's been a great 22 days. Board your flight home to the States in Brisbane this afternoon. You'll reach the U.S. West Coast only 1½ hours after leaving Australia, thanks to the International Date Line. The longest day of your life was custom-made for savoring those great Australian memories.

ARRIVE IN SYDNEY

Welcome to Australia! This is your first day Down Under, but you have many more to come, so don't exhaust yourself too quickly. You will arrive in Sydney in the morning. After clearing customs and immigration, travel into the city, get set in your hotel, refresh yourself, then spend the afternoon on a leisurely cruise of the beautiful Sydney Harbour.

Suggested Schedule

6:30-9:30	Arrive at Sydney Airport.
7:30-10:30	Take a bus into the city.
8:15-11:15	Get set up in your accommodation.
12:30	Lunch.
2:00	Sydney Harbour "Coffee Cruise" from Circular Quay. Or take a ferry to Manly.
5:00	Return to hotel.
6:30	Dinner in Darlinghurst.
9:00	Collapse into bed.

Airport Orientation

Kingsford Smith (Sydney) International Airport is located about 10 km south of the city center on Botany Bay. (Start thinking in metrics as soon as you arrive: 10 kilometers is about 6 miles.) When your plane drops in over the bay, you'll be arriving Down Under at almost the exact place as Captain James Cook, the first European to visit Australia, in 1770. Unlike Cook, you'll have to clear immigration and customs. Cap'n Jim was fortunate not to have to go through those formalities two centuries ago.

Travelers unlucky enough to arrive at the same time as a half-dozen other international flights will disagree, but I've always found the immigration procedures relatively painless here. Hopefully, you'll zoom through quickly, wait a few minutes to pluck your luggage from the baggage carousels, then move straight through customs into the arrival hall.

Change some money into Australian dollars at the airport bank, to the right. The rate here isn't quite as good as you'll find at the banks in the city, but the hotel counters are open to meet all incoming international flights; and if you've followed my suggestion and arrived on a Saturday, you'll need enough cash to get you through the weekend. (At this writing, I was getting

A$1.24 to US$1 at the airport, A$1.26 in town. Incidentally, some banks charge as much as A$5 commission for transactions; others assess no commission. Inquire before you exchange.)

At the south end of the arrival hall (farthest from the bank) is the Travellers Information Service desk. Here you can obtain hotel reservations, maps, and information on tourist attractions in Sydney and book a shuttle-bus ticket into town. A bus ticket, which entitles you to be dropped off at most hotels within the City Centre-Kings Cross area, costs A$3. Taxis run about A$12. Turn a cold shoulder on the rental car agents for now: you don't need one in the city. Public transportation is excellent, and you'll save a lot of money, not to mention parking and driving hassles, if you wait to pick up a car until you leave Sydney in three days.

If you haven't yet booked your domestic flight segments, take the escalator upstairs to the departure hall and do it now. If you are using Ansett Airlines' "Go-Australia" Plan, take Ansett Flight 200 from Melbourne to Alice Springs at 7:25 a.m. on Day 11; Ansett NT Flight BT278 from Alice Springs to Ayers Rock at 11:00 a.m. on Day 12; Ansett Flight 285 from Alice Springs to Cairns at 10:55 a.m. on Day 16; and Ansett Flight 39 from Cairns to Brisbane at 5:15 p.m. on Day 19.

Sydney Orientation
Over 20 percent of all Australians live in metropolitan Sydney. These 3½ million lucky people make their homes in one of the great cities on earth. It has everything they might ask for: a beautiful setting around a long, deep-blue harbor, a rich and varied cultural life, restaurants and hotels to suit all tastes and spending abilities, activities enough to support a book that could be entitled *22 Days in Sydney*.

Not only is Sydney Australia's largest city; it was also its first. On January 26, 1788, Captain Arthur Phillip arrived in Port Jackson (Sydney Harbour) with his "First Fleet" of 11 ships. He landed close to the site of the modern Harbour Bridge and established a settlement in the area known today as The Rocks. Nearly three-quarters of his 1,030 passengers were convicts, most of them deported from the British Isles for petty thievery, forgery, and similarly trumped-up charges. They became the foundation of the colony and the nation, and it is their success that Australia celebrated in its Bicentennial observance in 1988.

The oldest buildings standing in Sydney today are a legacy of Governor Lachlan Macquarie (1809-1821), who set an egalitarian standard for Australia by ordering the emancipation of deserving convicts to give them a "fair go" alongside free settlers. Yet it

Metropolitan Sydney

TO NEWCASTLE & BRISBANE

Broken Bay

Berowra Waters

Palm Beach

KU-RING-GAI CHASE
NATIONAL PARK

Newport

Dural

Terrey Hills

HORNSBY

Narrabeen

Pymble

Frenchs Forest

Dee Why

Baulkham Hills

Epping

Chatswood

Carlingford

Lane Cove

Cremorne

MANLY

PARRAMATTA

N. Sydney

Mosman

Watson Bay

Taronga Pk. Zoo

Vaucluse

Flemington

Leichhardt

Balmain

SYDNEY

Paddington

Regents Pk.

Chippendale

Bondi Junction

HUME-HWY.

Glebe

Bondi

Dulwich Hill

Randwick

BANKSTOWN

Wiley Park

Mascot

Coogee

Revesby

Kingsford
Smith Airport

HURSTVILLE

BOTANY BAY

Captain Cook's
Landing Site

SUTHERLAND

Cronulla

ROYAL
NATIONAL PARK

TO BLUE MTNS.

TO MELBOURNE

TO CANBERRA

TO WOLLONGONG

wasn't until the twentieth century, first with Commonwealth status ("independence") in 1901 and later with an influx of European immigrants, that the city really boomed.

Sydney's climate is similar to that of Los Angeles—without the smog. The mean summer temperature (December to February) is 78 degrees Fahrenheit; the winter mean (June to August) is 55 degrees. Average annual rainfall is 47.5 inches, with June the rainiest month (5.1 inches) and September the driest (0.6 inch). With such a comfortable climate, Sydneysiders love the outdoors. On most weekends and sunny afternoons you'll find them on their boats in the harbor or spangling the many fine beaches.

Though Sydney sprawls for many miles around the harbor, it's easy to find your way around the central area. Circular Quay, where ferries and cruise boats dock, is your point of orientation. East of the Quay, jutting into the harbor on Bennelong Point, is the Opera House, and immediately south of it the botanic gardens and The Domain. Macquarie Street is the main north-south thoroughfare here. West of the Quay, George and Pitt streets run from The Rocks (at the foot of the Harbour Bridge) through the City Centre to Chinatown and the central railway station. Park Street (becoming William Street) intersects George and Pitt streets at Sydney Town Hall and proceeds east, dissecting Hyde Park and running about a mile to Kings Cross. The Martin Place pedestrian hall, halfway between Park Street and Circular Quay, spans five blocks from George Street to Macquarie Street.

City Transportation

Between the subway/train, the monorail, and the bus and ferry system, Sydney is extremely well served by all forms of public transportation.

The Sydney Metropolitan Rail System (tel. 214-1067) serves 176 stations in nine lines running west, south, north, and east of Central Station. The City Circle subway line runs continuously from 5:00 a.m. to midnight between Museum, St. James, Circular Quay, Wynyard, Town Hall, and Central stations; the Eastern Suburbs line connects Town Hall with Martin Place, Kings Cross, and on to Bondi Junction. Systemwide maps can be obtained from any visitor information center. Standard fares for short distances are A$1. The new TNT Harbourlink monorail (tel. 552-2288) connects city center stations with Darling Harbour at a cost of A$2 per trip.

Buses of the Urban Transit Authority of New South Wales (tel. 954-9422) serve every corner of the metropolis that the trains miss. Fares start at A$1.10. A free bus service (No. 777) operates in the central city area at 10-minute intervals from 9:30 a.m. to 3:30 p.m. Monday to Friday. Another free bus (No. 666) connects Wynyard station with the Art Gallery of New South Wales in The Domain. Tourists are well served by the Sydney Explorer, a bright red double-decker bus that runs an 18-km loop to 20 major attractions for a set fee of A$10. The service operates continuously from 9:30 a.m. to 5:00 p.m. daily at 15-minute intervals.

The Urban Transit Authority also operates the ferry service from Circular Quay (tel. 29-2622) between 6:00 a.m. and 11:00 p.m. daily. The one-way fare is A$2.20 west to Hunters Hill and Greenwich, or across the harbor to Mosman, Cremorne, and Neutral Bay. To Manly, near the head of the harbor, it costs A$3 by ferry or A$4 by hydrofoil.

A special weekly ticket lets travelers take advantage of all transportation systems for a reduced cost. It can be purchased at the main railway station for A$12.

Where to Stay

Sydney's best hotels are a boomerang's throw from Circular Quay and The Rocks. **The Regent of Sydney**, 199 George St. (tel. 238-0000), is ranked among the world's elite: it's very expensive. . .but worth every penny, I'm told. Just down the street, and a small step down in price, is the **Old Sydney Parkroyal**, right in The Rocks at 55 George St. (tel. 20524). A well-entrenched favorite is the **Sheraton Wentworth**, 61 Phillip St. (tel. 230-0700).

For lower-cost lodging, the best selection is in Kings Cross, Sydney's answer to London's Soho and Paris' Pigalle. There's a lot of bustle and sleaze (some call it "character") here but no real danger as long as you mind your own business. In the moderate price bracket, check out the **Merlin Plaza**, a self-catering apartment hotel at 2 Springfield Ave. (tel. 356-3255).

For real budget accommodations, look on Victoria Street and Hughes Street, where you'll pay as little as A$10 a night in a dorm (perhaps A$20 a night in a shared double room) at a dozen small private hotels and backpackers' hostels. There's not a lot to choose between these places; I opt for the places with TV and rec rooms, not to mention good travelers' bulletin boards. Try **The Traveler's Rest**, 156 Victoria St. (tel. 358-4606), or **The Downunder Hostel**, 25 Hughes St. (tel. 358-1143). No hostel in the Cross is a member of the International Youth Hostel Federation; there are IYH hostels farther out at 262 Glebe Point Road, Glebe (tel. 692-8418); 28 Ross St., Forest Lodge (tel. 692-0747), near Sydney University; and 407 Marrickville Road, Dulwich Hill (tel. 569-0272).

Where to Eat
The best restaurant strip in Sydney, both in terms of price and
variety of cuisine, is Oxford Street in Darlinghurst, less than 1
km south of Kings Cross via Darlinghurst Road or Victoria
Street. For less than A$15 per person, you can eat well at such
diverse ethnic eateries as **Raquel's Ole Madrid** (Spanish, No.
145), **La Bella Notte** (Italian, No. 201), the **Balkan** (Greek, No.
209-215), **Momotaro** (Japanese, No. 225), **Kim** (No. 235, Vietnamese) or **Borobudur** (Indonesian, No. 263), among many
others. Around the corner and down the street are Sydney's
best selections for budget-watchers—**No Name** (that's what
locals call it; it really doesn't have a name), 2 Chapel St., a half-
block south of Stanley Street off Crown Street, and the **Metro
Cafe**, 26 Burton St. west of Crown. At either, you can get simple
but huge pasta-and-salad meals for around A$10. Two doors
down from the Metro on Burton is the **Different Drummer**, a
licensed establishment (the others are all BYO) in a lovely garden setting where steak or seafood dinners run A$10 to A$15.
Laurie's, opposite Green Park at Victoria and Burton streets,
has innovative vegetarian cuisine.
    In the Cross, you'll get a tasty if pricey meal at the upscale
Bayswater Brasserie, 32 Bayswater Road. Other moderate-
priced options: **Majit's Renamed Amar's**, 69 Macleay St., for
Indian curries, and **Benny's**, 12-14 Challis Ave., for Japanese
and Malay cuisine.
    Downtown, you can dine like an affluent tourist at the **Ben-
nelong Restaurant** in the Opera House, or in higher style yet
in the revolving restaurants atop **Sydney Tower** or **Australia
Square** (which is round, incidentally). More popular among
locals in a moderate price range are **Johnny Walker's Bistro** in
Angel Place (near Martin Place) for steaks; the **Sorrento**, 5
Elizabeth St. (basement), for seafood; **The Old Spaghetti Factory**, 80 George St., The Rocks, for pasta and atmosphere; **Pan-
cakes on the Rocks**, 10 Hickson Road, for 24-hour munchies;
and the **Imperial Peking Harbourside**, 15 Circular Quay
West, for upmarket Chinese food.
    If you want to eat like the Asians, though, visit the
Chinatown Food Fair, Dixon and Goulburn streets (third
floor). Open from 11:00 a.m. to 11:00 p.m. daily (to 9:00 p.m.
Sundays), you can sate your appetite for under A$5 while
choosing your meal from over a dozen Southeast Asia-style
food stalls. There's a smaller version of same at **Dixon Gour-
met**, Dixon and Little Hay streets. Away from Sydney's core,
two restaurants deserve a special mention. **Doyle's on the
Beach**, at Watson's Bay near the south head of the harbor
mouth, is so famous for its seafood that it runs a special shuttle

ferry from a dock near Circular Quay. The **Berowra Waters Inn**, Berowra, is considered the best of all possible restaurants in Australia. To get there, you must drive an hour north from the city center to a jetty, where you are met by a private punt. It's open Friday to Sunday only, and bookings are required.

Helpful Hints
The **Sydney Visitors Bureau** (tel. 235-2424) is in Martin Place at Elizabeth Street, smack in the middle of downtown. The office provides maps and brochures and books seats for tours or entertainment events, 9:00 a.m. to 5:00 p.m. weekdays.

The **General Post Office** is also on Martin Place at the corner of Pitt Street. Banks are open 9:30 a.m. to 4:00 p.m. Monday to Thursday, 9:30 a.m. to 5:00 p.m. Friday. Most shops are open from 9:00 a.m. to 5:30 p.m. Monday to Wednesday, 9:00 a.m. to 9:00 p.m. Thursday and Friday, 9:00 a.m. to 12:00 noon Saturday.

There's a **U.S. Consulate General** in the T&G Building, Elizabeth and Park streets (tel. 261-9200), and a **Canadian Consulate General** on the 8th Floor of the AMP Centre, 50 Bridge St. (tel. 231-6522).

In case of emergencies, dial 000.

AROUND SYDNEY

Today is devoted to exploring the major sights of the city's core. Take the red double-decker bus, the Sydney Explorer (see "City Transportation," Day 1), or—better yet—walk.

Suggested Schedule

8:00	Breakfast at hotel.
9:00	Take the bus, subway or walk to the Opera House, arriving for the guided tour.
10:30	Experience the view from Sydney Tower.
11:15	Browse through Hyde Park Barracks and The Old Mint.
12:30	Picnic lunch in The Domain or Botanic Gardens.
1:30	Art Gallery of N.S.W.
3:00	Australian Museum.
4:30	The Rocks: start a walking tour at the visitor center, but dawdle in the shops and pubs.
7:30	Dinner and show at the Argyle Tavern.

Sightseeing Highlights
▲▲▲ **Sydney Harbour** (see Day 1)—Life in Sydney centers on the Harbour. Thirteen miles (21 km) long from its ocean heads to the mouth of the Paramatta River, with some 160 miles (250 km) of crenellated coastline, the deep blue inlet seems permanently speckled with boats of all sizes and shapes. On sunny weekend afternoons, the colorful jibs of myriad sailboats make the harbor look like a seaborne carnival. The Opera House and Harbour Bridge are its unmistakable landmarks, but there is much more to see: colonial mansions and modern architectural showcases, the skylines of downtown and North Sydney, the laughing face and looming roller coaster of Luna Park, the sandstone turrets of Fort Denison on venerable Pinchgut Island.

All Harbour cruises leave the city from Circular Quay, at the foot of Pitt Street. Ferry routes and fares are discussed in Day 1 under "City Transportation." There's also a Sydney Harbour Explorer: for a flat fee of A$14, you can spend the day shuttling between the Opera House, The Rocks, Pier 1, the Taronga Park Zoo, and Watson Bay. The Explorer leaves Circular Quay hourly each day from 9:30 a.m. to 3:30 p.m. One-hour stopovers are permitted, with free reboarding.

There are several cruise operators. I like Captain Cook Cruises, with 14 tour options daily from 9:00 a.m. to 7:30 p.m., varying in length from 75 minutes to six hours and in price from A\$9 to A\$41.50. A good introductory trip is the Captain Cook Coffee Cruise, leaving Pier 6 every day at 10:00 a.m. and 2:00 p.m. The 2 ½ -hour trip includes refreshments.

▲▲▲**Sydney Opera House**, Bennelong Point. One of the

most unique buildings on Earth, the Opera House was designed
by Danish architect Jorn Utzon, begun in 1959 and opened in
1973. Talk about inflation: its cost was first estimated at A$7 mil-
lion, but it wound up costing A$102 million! It's really much
more than a stage for operas; the complex also contains a concert hall, drama and movie theaters, a recording hall, an exhibition hall, two restaurants, six lounges, a library and archives,
and various rehearsal studios, dressing rooms, and administra-
tive offices, all under the distinctive saillike roofs.

Sixty-minute guided tours are conducted daily (except Good
Friday and Christmas) from 9:00 a.m. to 4:00 p.m. Backstage
tours, lasting 90 minutes, are offered Sundays only. They start
from the Music Room-Exhibition foyer on the ground level;
tickets are A$3.50.

A better way to appreciate the Opera House is to take in a performance. You can get a full schedule of all events at most visitor centers. The Opera House box office is open Monday to
Saturday from 9:00 a.m. to 8:30 p.m. and Sunday from 9:00
a.m. to 4:00 p.m. You can also book by phone (with a major
credit card) by calling 20525.

▲▲**Sydney Tower** rises 1,000 feet above the Centrepoint
shopping complex off Market Street between Pitt and Castle-
reagh streets. Some Aussie cynics call this edifice "the bucket on
the stick," but as the highest public building in the Southern
Hemisphere, it's worth the trip up for the view. Open 9:30 a.m.
to 9:30 p.m. Monday to Saturday, 10:30 a.m. to 4:30 p.m. Sunday and public holidays; closed Christmas. It will cost you
A$3.50 to take the lift up. Lunch and dinner are served in a pair
of restaurants immediately below the observation deck.

▲▲ **Hyde Park Barracks** is on Queen's Square at the top of
Macquarie Street. Designed by convict architect Francis Green-
way (whose picture is on the A$10 bill) and erected in 1819 as a
dormitory for male convicts, it has become an interesting
museum of Sydney social history. Start on the top floor to learn
in considerable detail about the shipment of convicts from
England to Sydney, then step down to the second floor to trace
the city's nineteenth-century development. Open 10:00 a.m. to
5:00 p.m. daily (noon to 5:00 p.m. Tuesday); closed Good Friday and Christmas. Free admission.

▲**The Old Mint** is next door to the Barracks. One of Australia's
oldest public buildings (1817), it was built as a hospital wing but
became the first branch of the British Royal Mint outside of London after gold was discovered in 1851. Since 1982, it has been
an elegant, well-organized museum of decorative art, coins, and
stamps. Open 10:00 a.m. to 5:00 p.m. daily (noon to 5:00 p.m.

Wednesday); closed Good Friday and Christmas. Free admission.

▲ **Art Gallery of New South Wales**, Art Gallery Road, The Domain—Sydney's (but not Australia's) best art museum, it is interesting for its survey of Aussie paintings through the nineteenth and twentieth centuries. A major 1987-88 expansion added a sculpture terrace, Asian art gallery, and several theaters. Open 10:00 a.m. to 5:00 p.m. daily (noon to 5:00 p.m. Sunday); closed Good Friday and Christmas. Free admission.

▲ **Royal Botanic Gardens**—The second botanic gardens in the Southern Hemisphere are a pleasant place for a stroll or a picnic. Open 8:00 a.m. to sunset daily. Free guided walks are conducted at 9:30 a.m. Wednesday and 10:00 a.m. Friday from the visitor center.

▲▲ **The Australian Museum**, located at the corner of William and College streets (opposite Hyde Park), is of special interest for superb exhibits of Aboriginal and Papua New Guinean lifestyles. It also has good displays of Australian geological and natural history, as well as a Pacific art gallery. Open 10:00 a.m. to 5:00 p.m. daily (noon to 5:00 p.m. Monday); closed Good Friday and Christmas. Free admission.

▲▲ **Darling Harbour**, a 133-acre urban redevelopment project on the west end of downtown Sydney, opened in 1988 to acclaim. Connected by monorail to the city center, it is built around a central park and Chinese garden and includes a convention and exhibition center, a hotel/casino, 30 restaurants, 200 retail shops, and an entertainment center. Also within the complex are **Sydney Aquarium**, which claims to be the world's largest, and the **Australian National Maritime Museum**.

▲▲ **The Powerhouse**, adjacent to Darling Harbour at Harris and Mary Ann streets in Ultimo, is an impressive science and technology museum that also opened for the Bicentennial in 1988. Displays—many of them hands-on—cover everything from steam engines to the space race to the history of the brewing industry in New South Wales. Open 10:00 a.m. to 5:00 p.m. daily.

▲ **Elizabeth Bay House**, Onslow Avenue, Elizabeth Bay. Close to Kings Cross but on the Sydney Explorer bus route, this elegant 1835 colonial mansion has been fully restored to period decor. Open 10:00 a.m. to 4:30 p.m. Tuesday through Sunday. Adult admission $2.50; Sydney Explorer patrons $2.

▲▲▲ **The Rocks**—Sydney's most historic district is located just northwest of Circular Quay. The oldest building still standing, Cadmans Cottage, was built in 1816, but most structures date from the 1840s to 1880s, during which time this was Sydney's main commercial and maritime quarter.

To see the area properly, you should guide yourself on a walking tour beginning from the Rocks Visitor Centre, 104 George St.—open Monday to Friday 8:30 a.m. to 4:30 p.m., weekends and holidays 10:00 a.m. to 5:00 p.m. You can pick up a map describing various sites, but the best way to explore is simply to amble and browse, ducking into the various small shops, art galleries, museums, and pubs. Several pubs, including The Old Push, Phillips Foote, and the venerable Hero of Waterloo, feature live "trad jazz" performances during after-work "happy hour" and on weekends.

The highlight of The Rocks is the **Argyle Centre**, a four-story complex of various artisans' galleries, antique shops, and cafés. Housed in a group of 1828 sandstone bond stores and warehouses, it authentically preserves the atmosphere of the period—and nowhere better than the **Argyle Tavern**, a great spot for an Australian night out. As you fill up on Sydney rock oysters, grilled barramundi, or steak-and-kidney pie, the Jolly Swagman Show will introduce you to a variety of Aussie bush ballads and folk songs, the Aboriginal didgeridoo (a primitive droning instrument), and the fine art of shearing a sheep—right on stage. Showtime is 8:00 to 9:30 nightly; come by 7:30 to place your order and beat the rush. A warning: shoestring travelers may want to think twice before purging their wallets of A$50 (per person) for the dinner and show.

MORE OF SYDNEY

I'd spend today touring the Eastern Suburbs, but there are many other options—take the ferry to Manly and the zoo, for instance, or travel to the Blue Mountains or the Hunter Valley.

Suggested Schedule	
9:00	Take the subway (Blue Line) to Bondi Junction, then catch Bus No. 380 or 389 to Bondi Beach. You'll arrive by 9:30 a.m., giving you two hours to soak in rays and surf culture before lunch.
11:30	Catch a city bus north up the coast to Watson's Bay for a seafood lunch at Doyle's.
1:30	Bus No. 325 heads back toward the city. Stop off at Vaucluse House, an 1830s mansion.
2:30	Disembark in Double Bay for a look at Sydney's version of Rodeo Drive.
3:30	Have a cab drop you in Paddington at the New Edition Bookshop, 328 Oxford St., where you can obtain free "The Paddington Book" with a map and suggested walking tour.
5:30	Continue to the Cross by foot, bus, or taxi. It's your night to paint the town red.

Sightseeing Highlights

▲▲**Bondi** (pronounced Bond-eye) is the most famous of all Sydney's beaches. It's not the most attractive, unless perhaps you're talking about the topless south end of the beach; but there seems to be more tradition and a livelier crowd here than at other Eastern Suburbs beaches, especially during summer when surf livesaving contests are held throughout Australia.

▲**Vaucluse House**, Olala Avenue, Vaucluse, was built in 1803 and became the home of William Charles Wentworth, the Thomas Jefferson of Australia, from 1827 to 1853. A beachfront manor that sits in 27 acres of park and garden, it has been lavishly refurbished in the style of Wentworth's time. Open 10:00 a.m. to 4:30 p.m. Tuesday to Sunday. Adult admission is $2.50.

▲**Double Bay** may be Australia's most fashionable few blocks. Knox Street, Cross Street, and New South Head Road are lined with designer boutiques, exclusive jewelers, and antique shops.

You'll see Sydney's beautiful people sizing each other up at sidewalk cafés and delis.

▲▲**Paddington** may be downmarket from Double Bay, but it's upmarket from most of the rest of Sydney. Known locally as "Paddo," this hilly neighborhood might strike Washingtonians as being a little like Georgetown. Here, the young, upwardly mobile population has put its restoration energies into Victorian terrace houses rather than brownstone manors. Many artists, musicians, and educators live among the trendy arts and crafts galleries and numerous fine restaurants and pubs.

Special attractions in Paddington include an open-air market called the **Village Bazaar**, held from 9:00 a.m. to 4:00 p.m. every Saturday at the corner of Newcombe and Oxford Street, and the **Victoria Barracks**, a superb example of British colonial military architecture on Oxford Street opposite Hopewell Street. If you're here on Tuesday, see the impressive changing of the guard at 11:00 a.m.

▲**Manly** is a good destination for those who prefer to spend time on the water instead of in trains and buses. Spread across a narrow neck of land separating the Harbour from the Tasman Sea, it has a quaint pedestrian mall connecting the famed surfing beach with a still-water swimming area. Manly's attractions include a Marineland (open 10:00 a.m. to 5:00 p.m. daily), an amusement pier, a series of waterslides, and an art gallery/museum. Manly is easily reached from Circular Quay by ferry (A$3 each way) or hydrofoil (A$4 each way).

▲**Taronga Park Zoo**, Bradleys Head Road, Mosman, is an excellent place to get an introduction to Australia's unique wildlife. Its exhibits include a treetop koala exhibit, a platypus house, a rain-forest aviary, and a special nocturnal house. You can travel there either by ferry from Circular Quay (A$2.20 each way) or by Bus No. 237 or 238 across the Sydney Harbour Bridge. Open daily year-round, 9:00 a.m. to 5:00 p.m. Admission is $5.

Birkenhead Point, a shopping center off Victoria Road in the harborside suburb of Drummoyne, a few miles west of the city center, might be considered a rainy-day option. There are some 130 shops and restaurants, plus the **Lego Centre**, one of only two permanent exhibitions in the world of models built from these childhood building blocks. Open daily 9:15 a.m. to 5:15 p.m., Thursdays until 9:00 p.m.

Day Trips from Sydney
If you're inclined to rent your car a day early, here are some worthwhile day trip options.

▲**The Blue Mountains**, once a foreboding natural barrier to early settlers, are now a favorite weekend getaway for Sydney-siders. Their undeclared capital is Katoomba, a small town 106 km (66 miles) west of Sydney, though they spread from Penrith to Lithgow. The mountains' most famous attraction is **The Three Sisters**, an unusual rock formation associated with Aboriginal legend. A cable car and scenic railway at the site make it a honeymooners' delight. There are also spectacular caves and waterfalls, art galleries, and historic museums.

▲**Pittwater** and **Broken Bay**, at the mouth of the Hawkesbury River marking the northern boundary of the Sydney metropolis, are places of great natural beauty. They're best seen from the deck of a private yacht, but they can also be thoroughly·appreciated from the land. Drive north up Sydney's east coast through Mona Vale to **Palm Beach**, or better yet, spend an afternoon bushwalking in **Ku-ring-gai Chase National Park**.

▲**Old Sydney Town**, near Gosford about 70 km (43 miles) north of downtown Sydney, re-creates the Sydney Cove settlement as it is thought to have been in the early 1800s. Only authentic materials and methods were used in building the 50-acre theme park. Soldiers, convicts, and free settlers, all in period costume, continually act out scenes from the colony's history. Open 10:00 a.m. to 5:00 p.m. Wednesday to Sunday; daily during school holidays. Admission is A$10.80. A rail tour, leaving Sydney's Central Station at 8:09 a.m. and returning shortly after 6:05 p.m., costs A$23 for adults and includes admission.

▲**The Hunter Valley**, near Cessnock some 180 km (110 miles) north of Sydney, is Australia's oldest wine-producing district and its second most important (after the Barossa Valley near Adelaide). The 34 wineries here are best known for their soft reds. Most are open for tasting daily from 9:00 or 10:00 a.m. to about 5:00 p.m. Hungerford Hill, Rothbury Estate, Tyrrells, and Wyndham Estate are among the most highly regarded.

Nightlife
Anything and everything goes in **Kings Cross**, several meandering blocks of burlesque shows, theater restaurants, discotheques, tattoo parlors, and streetwalkers where Darlinghurst Road, Victoria Street, Bayswater Road, and William Street come together a mile east of the city center. Some call the Cross "bohemian," others "sleazy"; the truth may lie somewhere between. People-watching is the best form of entertainment here; grab a window table and a cup of cappuccino at an open-

air café. You might also get a kick out of the automated Ray Charles double playing piano and singing at **Jo Jo Ivory's** in the Potts Point Sheraton, 40 Macleay St.

To find out what's happening on any given day in the greater Sydney area, get hold of *The Sydney Morning Herald*'s Friday "Metro" section, with listings of the entertainment week ahead. Musical offerings are broken down into classical, jazz, country, folk, acoustic, and rock, with the latter category as large as the other five combined. Paddington (try the **Grand National Hotel** or the **Windsor Castle Hotel**) and Bondi (the **Royal Hotel** is best) have especially large concentrations of music pubs, but you'll find them everywhere.

The best modern jazz in Sydney is consistently found at **The Basement**, 29 Reiby Place near Circular Quay. For good rock in a trendy atmosphere, check out the **Oz Rock Cafe**, 248 William St., Kings Cross, or the ubiquitous **Hard Rock Cafe**, 121 Crown St., Darlinghurst.

If you're strictly into meeting people without having to shout over the din of music, check out some of the city's wine bars— like **French's** on Oxford Street in Darlinghurst, **Soren's** in Woolloomooloo, or **The Stoned Crow** in Crow's Nest, across the Harbour Bridge. In North Sydney you'll also find **Sheila's**, a singles bar with provocative coasters that read, "If you're looking for a friend, leave this side up."

Live theater is extremely popular in Sydney. Aside from the Opera House, you can take in fine productions at **The Theatre Royal** on King Street, **The Wharf Theatre** on Pier 4 (near The Rocks), and others. Lower George Street has the greatest concentration of cinema houses for moviegoers. All major studio American films are shown here, but don't miss an opportunity to see some of the outstanding movies made in Australia today.

An Australian phenomenon is the Leagues Club, of which rugby league clubs and returned servicemen's league clubs are most prevalent. Depending upon their size, they usually include a small gambling casino (with slot machines), a restaurant and bar, and an entertainment lounge, often with live music on weekends. This is where the working man typically takes his wife or girlfriend for a night out. While they are memberships clubs, overseas visitors are normally welcome. Two of the biggest are the **South Sydney Junior Rugby League Club**, 556 Anzac Parade, Kingsford, and the **St. George Leagues Club**, 124 Princes Highway, Kogarah.

SYDNEY TO CANBERRA

Leave Australia's queen city and drive south to Canberra, the national capital, pausing en route at historic Gledswood Homestead and Berrima. In Canberra, take time for an overview of the foundation and continuing evolution of this attractive, specially created city.

Suggested Schedule

8:00	Pick up your reserved rental car and head out of Sydney via the Hume Highway.
9:30	Arrive at Gledswood Homestead and wander through the working colonial farm.
10:45	Leave for Berrima.
11:30	Explore Berrima, a sandstone-and-brick village appearing very much today as it did in 1831. Lunch at the Surveyor General Inn, the oldest continuously licensed pub in Australia.
1:30	Leave for Canberra.
3:30	On arrival, drive straight to the Regatta Point Planning Exhibition on Lake Burley Griffin. Study the models and see the video to understand the grand plan for this twentieth-century capital.
4:30	Capture the view from the top of Mount Ainslie.
5:00	Move into your accommodation. Plan on a quiet evening; most of them are just that in Canberra.

Leaving Sydney

When you obtain your rental car, double-check to be certain your agent has provided you with a Gregory's or UBD street guide to Sydney. That's your passport out of the metropolis in case you get lost.

Most visitors get their car at a rental agent on William Street, between Kings Cross and downtown. Proceed west through Hyde Park, turn left on Pitt Street, and follow the signs to Liverpool. The Hume Highway, Route 31, branches south (to the left) off the Great Western Highway near Summer Hill, 8 km from William Street.

The Hume Highway
Soon after leaving Liverpool, about 30 km from the Hume Highway junction, the highway becomes a four-lane freeway. It stays
that way (with only a couple of slowdowns) all the way to
Canberra—in fact, to Melbourne—enabling you to drive the
294 km (183 miles) from Sydney to the capital in 3 ½ hours, if
you so choose.

Our tour route, however, involves a few diversions. At the
point where the freeway begins, turn right on Route 89, Cam-
den Valley Way (the old Hume Highway), to the community of
Catherine Field. It's about 10 km farther to the historic **Gledswood Homestead**, built in 1810 by convict labor and now classified by the National Trust and the Heritage Commission.
Guided tours of the homestead, winery (in a former coach
house), and working farm are offered daily from 9:00 a.m. to
5:00 p.m. Sheep shearing, boomerang throwing, and other
demonstrations are often presented.

▲▲**Berrima** is bypassed by the new freeway, making its
colonial isolation all the more appealing. Situated 128 km (80
miles) from Sydney and 166 km (103 miles) from Canberra, this
village (founded in 1831) is a historical gem. Pick up a walking
tour map at the Georgian-style **courthouse**, where the first
jury trial in the New South Wales colony was held in 1843. (It's
open 10:00 a.m. to 4:00 p.m. daily; admission is A60 cents.) The
jail, built in 1839, closed in 1902 but reopened in 1949 after
extensive reconstruction (and still in use), was one of the most
feared in Australia in the mid-nineteenth century.

About two dozen government buildings, early churches, and
private manors have survived the passage of time. Many of them
may contain galleries, antique and crafts shops, and restaurants
and cafés serving Devonshire teas. At the **Surveyor General
Inn**, which celebrates its 156th anniversary in business in 1990,
you can cook your own steak lunch, pile it high with a salad bar
and potatoes, and wash it down with a beer for under A$10.

A further diversion off the Hume Highway from Berrima
would lead you through the charming village of **Bundanoon** at
the edge of lush Morton National Park. Time's a-wastin', however. Return to the freeway, drive right on through the big farming center of Goulburn (pop. 25,000), waving at the campy
"world's largest Merino sheep" sculpture as you pass. Twelve
km farther on, bear left onto the Federal Highway and slide by
the rim of large (but usually dry) Lake George into the Australian
Capital Territory.

Canberra Orientation
Visitors often find Canberra like a tree without roots, a building
without a foundation. Indeed, the city is too young to have

developed much heritage of its own. Like Washington, D.C., Canberra, A.C.T., is strictly a government town—but its 250,000 people haven't had a 187-year history to develop a feeling of heritage. It wasn't until 1901 that Melbourne and Sydney, throwing up their political arms in frustration over persistent squabbling for the right to be the national capital, finally compromised and agreed to construct a new city between the two metropolises.

In 1912, an American architect named Walter Burley Griffin won an international contest to design the capital. Following his plans, 2,366 square km (913 square miles) of sheep-grazing land were transformed into the Australian Capital Territory, and within that plot, the new city of Canberra was built. (The name "Canberra" was derived from an Aboriginal term meaning "meeting place.") In 1927, all government functions were moved here from Melbourne.

Burley Griffin's grandiose plan has taken far longer to complete than anyone imagined. Between two world wars, a Great Depression, and much political infighting, construction funds have been hard to come by. In fact, Canberra is only now being completed to the architect's specifications! After 60 years of legislative debates in a provisional parliament house, a magnificent new Parliament House was finished just in time for the Australian Bicentennial in 1988.

Canberra's design carefully balances natural features—low, bush-cloaked mountains and lovely, meandering Lake Burley Griffin—with geometrical patterns, mainly a series of concentric circles interconnected by strong lines. Capitol Hill, site of the new Parliament, and City Hill, around which most commercial functions revolve, are 3 km apart, linked across the deep blue lake by Commonwealth Avenue. Each "hill" is the hub of a series of streets that spread from the center like the spokes of a wheel.

Northbourne Avenue, on which you'll arrive from the north, runs straight as an arrow for over 4 km directly to City Hill. Soon after you circumnavigate the hill but before crossing the lake, look for directional signs to the **Canberra Planning Exhibition** on Regatta Point, operated by the National Capital Development Commission. Put preconceived notions aside; if you have any interest in the creative process, it isn't boring. In effect, it's a historical museum, describing with text, photographs, and audiovisual presentation the creation of Canberra from virtually uninhabited bush. A huge, three-dimensional model of the city helps you locate points of interest. Open 9:00 a.m. to 5:00 p.m. daily (except Christmas); admission is free. A snack bar and souvenir shop are on a terrace overlooking the lake.

Of several hills with lookouts over the city, the best—from the standpoint of understanding Canberra's layout—is **Mount Ainslie** in the northeast quadrant. Not only is it the highest at 842 meters (2,772 feet); from the top, you can look straight down across the stalwart Australian War Memorial to Anzac Parade, which neatly bisects the Federal Triangle and affords a direct view of the provisional and new Parliament Houses.

The highest viewpoint in Canberra is actually atop the striking 195-meter (640-foot) Telecom Tower on **Black Mountain** west of City Hill. But unless you dine in the revolving restaurant, you'll have to pay to gain access to the three public viewing galleries. Another lookout is on **Red Hill**, south of Capitol Hill, with a restaurant offering panoramic views of the southern suburbs.

Canberra's climate, quite logically, is unlike that of any of the seaside state capitals. Located about 120 km (75 miles) inland and at 580 meters (1,900 feet) elevation in a spur of the Great Dividing Range, its summers are hotter and drier than other major cities and its winters colder, with occasional (if rare) snow flurries.

City Transportation

If you arrive in Canberra without a car at the airport, railway depot, or bus station, you're not stranded. The ACTION public bus network runs through the city and its suburbs from 6:00 a.m. to 11:30 p.m. daily (8:30 a.m. to 6:30 p.m. Sunday), with fares of A60 cents to most destinations. No. 230 operates to Regatta Point and along the north shore of Lake Burley Griffin; No. 302 runs from the city to the Australian War Memorial; No. 357 connects City Hill with the rail station via the National Library and provisional Parliament House; No. 380 plies the 8 km (5 miles) between the youth hostel and downtown.

Better designed for the tourist is the Canberra Explorer. This unmistakable bright red bus runs its narrated 25-km (15½-mile) circuit 7 times every day from 9:40 a.m. to 4:35 p.m., making scheduled stops at major attractions and hotels. You can buy a day ticket for A$7, allowing you to disembark anywhere and reboard an hour or two later, or pay A$2.50 for a one-hour tour.

Where to Stay

The greatest concentration of accommodations in all price categories is along Northbourne Avenue, the main thoroughfare entering Canberra from the north. Regarded by some as the best is the **Canberra International**, 242 Northbourne Ave., Dickson, ACT 2602 (tel. 47-6966), with luxury rooms and a garden atmosphere. I'm happy in the moderate price range at **Down Town Spero's Motel**, 82 Northbourne Ave., Canberra, ACT 2601 (tel. 49-1388), an easy three-block stroll from the commercial center around City Hill.

You'll find adequate economy-class lodging at **Tall Trees Lodge**, Stephen and Sherbrooke streets, Ainslie, ACT 2602 (tel. 47-9200). The **Gowrie Private Hotel**, 210 Northbourne Ave., Braddon, ACT 2602 (tel. 49-6033), has twin 10-story towers containing 569 simple rooms and a big, round-floor cafeteria. True budget accommodations are hard to come by in Canberra, but the **National Memorial Youth Hostel** is on Dryandra Street in O'Connor, ACT 2601 (tel. 48-9759).

Where to Eat

The most central area for dining is Garema Place, a spacious pedestrian mall east of Northbourne Avenue and north of London Circuit, just above City Hill. There's a wide range of choices here, from candlelit meals to fast-food takeaway. **Dorette's Bistro**, upstairs at 17 Garema Place (near Bunda Street), is one of my favorites; it's a self-styled Bohemian café with live classical and jazz music on alternate nights. **Mama's Trattoria**, 7 Garema Place, offers big pasta meals for no more than A$7. A couple of blocks away is the 24-hour **Lovely Lady Pancake Parlour**, East Row and Alinga Street, with full meals A$5-$7 and a bottomless coffee cup. Not far away, near City Hill on Northbourne Avenue, **Boyd's Cafe** at No. 47 and the **Private Bin** at No. 50 offer bistro menus and entertainment. Vegetarians congregate at the **Honeydew Wholemeal**, 55 Northbourne Ave.

Downtown, upscale favorites among politicians and local businessmen are the **Fringe Benefits** brasserie, 54 Marcus Clarke St., and **Seasons**, in the Canberra Theatre Center, both serving continental cuisine.

Not far from Garema Place, on Lonsdale Street, **The Eureka Stockade** at No. 17 is a local favorite for steaks and beer. Opposite at No. 14-16 are the **Siamese Kitchen**, with spicy Southeast Asian cuisine for A$8-$10, and the **Tipsy Gypsy**, a Hungarian restaurant. Other ethnic restaurants in the Civic Centre area include Chinese, Indian, Vietnamese, and Lebanese.

Worthy of special note are **Tilley Devine's Cafe Gallery**, 96 Wattle St., Lynehan, a feminist-operated establishment that doesn't admit men unless accompanied by women; the **Tau**, on Mort Street directly behind **Spero's**, a vegetarian and Middle Eastern restaurant operated by a community theater group; the **Canberra Tradesmen's Union Club**, Badham Street, Dickson, with reasonably priced bistro meals served in restored

trams; and a pair of cafeterias in Australian National University's
student center, the **ANU Refectory** and the **Asian Bistro**.

Helpful Hints
The **Canberra Tourist Bureau** (tel. 45-6405 or 45-6464) has
its main offices in the Jolimont Centre on Northbourne Avenue
near London Circuit. It's open weekdays 8:30 a.m. to 5:15 p.m.
and Saturdays 9:00 to 11:30 a.m. More convenient for those
driving into town from the north is the **Visitor Information
Centre**, on Northbourne Avenue just south of the junctions of
the Federal and Barton highways, open daily (except Christmas)
from 9:00 a.m. to 5:00 p.m.

The **General Post Office** adjoins the Jolimont Centre at
Alinga and Moore streets. Banks open from 9:30 a.m. to 4:00
p.m. Monday to Thursday, an hour later on Friday. Shops are
generally open 9:00 a.m. to 5:30 p.m. Monday to Friday, 9:00
a.m. to 4:00 p.m. Saturday. (Some stay open later Friday nights
but close by noon Saturday.)

The elegant **U.S. Embassy** is at State Circle and Perth Avenue
in Yarralumla, near Capitol Hill (tel. 73-3711). The **Canadian
Embassy** is on Commonwealth Avenue (tel. 73-3844).

In case of emergencies, dial 000.

CANBERRA

Explore the national capital. Start at the new Parliament House;
if the Senate and House of Representatives are in session, you
can view the proceedings from a public gallery. Take a drive
through the Yarralumla area to see the impressive row of
national embassies, then lunch at the High Court, inspect the
National Gallery, and visit the Australian War Memorial
museum.

Suggested Schedule

9:00	View Australia's new Parliament House or preview it from the Exhibition Centre.
9:30	Get in line for a 10:00 a.m. session of the Senate or House of Representatives at the new Parliament House.
11:00	Drive through Canberra's "Embassy Row."
12:00 noon	Visit the High Court and have lunch in its café.
1:30	Peruse the Australian National Gallery.
3:00	Spend a couple hours at the Australian War Memorial Museum.
5:00	Hire a canoe for a trip on Lake Burley Griffin or return to your hotel and relax.
7:00	Dine in Garema Place.

Sightseeing Highlights
▲▲▲**The New Parliament House**, with its memorable A$4
million flagpole, was officially opened on May 9, 1988, by
Queen Elizabeth II. The designers—the American firm of
Mitchell/Giurgola and Australian architect Richard Thorp—kept
intact Walter Burley Griffin's original plan for Canberra with
gently curving walls and careful landscaping, picking up the
axis pattern of earlier roads and buildings. The 266-foot, four-
legged flagpole is intended to be the emblem of Australian government.

The building's architecture follows the circular contours of
Capitol Hill with curved walls and a grassy walkway over the
top of the gently sloping roof. The House of Representatives lies
on the east side of the walls, the Senate on the west. The main
public entry is from the north, past a ceremonial pool. Works of
Australian art are incorporated in the interior design, including
an Aboriginal mosaic in the Forecourt. All told, the massive

structure covers 79 acres and contains 450 separate rooms. It cost just over A$1,000 million to build.

Parliament is in session from March to November. Business is conducted in the traditional "Westminster" fashion, complete with powdered wigs. Sessions commence at 2:00 and 8:00 p.m. Monday and Tuesday, 10:00 a.m. and 2:00 p.m. Wednesday, 10:00 a.m. and 8:00 p.m. Thursday, and 9:00 a.m. (Senate) or 10:00 a.m. (House) and again at 2:00 p.m. on Friday. There's no admission, but you may need advance bookings to sit in the House's popular gallery. (Call 72-1211 or 72-6606 on arrival in Canberra.) Arrive a little early to get in line. You'll be admitted on a first-come, first-served basis; your visit will be limited to 25 minutes if there's a crowd waiting.

▲**The Provisional Parliament House**, never intended to be more than a temporary capitol, was the seat of Australia's federal goverment from 1927 to 1988. A graceful white building in a parklike setting on King George Terrace, it is now being converted to a constitutional museum. Inside is a gallery of oil portraits of Queen Elizabeth II, past governor-generals, and parliamentarians.

▲**Embassy Row** really doesn't exist as such, but the Yarralumla section of Canberra, just west of Capitol Hill, has the highest concentration of foreign embassies in Australia. Most are elegant edifices reflecting national architectural tastes and easily viewed from the winding residential roads. Few are open to visitors except on official business, but the Indonesian Embassy, 8 Darwin Ave., has a pavilion displaying crafts and musical instruments open daily from 10:00 a.m. to 12:30 p.m. and 2:00 to 4:00 p.m., and the High Commission of Papua New Guinea, Forster Crescent, has a display of trade and cultural items open weekdays from 9:00 a.m. to 12:30 p.m. and 2:30 to 4:30 p.m.

▲▲**The High Court of Australia**, in an impressive concrete-and-glass structure on the shore of Lake Burley Griffin, is the nation's ultimate court of appeal. The Great Hall—the main public area—has two huge murals depicting the justice system and the states. Ramps connect it with courtrooms on three succeeding floors, decorated with indigenous woodwork, woven tapestries, sculptures, and other native artworks. When in session, the court sits from 10:15 a.m. to 12:45 p.m. and 2:15 to 4:15 p.m. weekdays. The building is open to visitors 9:45 a.m. to 4:30 p.m. most days. A licensed café, overlooking Lake Burley Griffin, serves excellent light meals for A$5 or less.

▲▲**The Australian National Gallery**, connected by a first-floor walkway to the High Court building, has a fine if limited collection of Australian and foreign paintings, sculpture, and

decorative arts. Free guided tours of the Australian art section
are offered daily at 11:15 a.m. and 2:15 p.m. The gallery is open
10:00 a.m. to 5:00 p.m. daily except Good Friday and
Christmas; admission is A$2.

▲**The National Library of Australia**, west of the High Court
on the lakefront, has an Australian art collection of its own, displayed daily from 9:00 a.m. to 4:45 p.m. in the Rex Nan Kivell
Room. Some 3.6 million volumes of books are stored in 10 acres
of space and on 47 miles of shelves. The main reading room is
open to the public 9:30 a.m. to 10:00 p.m. Monday to Thursday,
9:30 a.m. to 4:45 p.m. Friday and Saturday, and 1:30 to 4:45
p.m. Sunday.

▲▲▲**The Australian War Memorial** is the country's best
museum of any kind. Whether you view war as glorious, horri-
ble, or a bit of both, this somber memorial will make a definite
impression. Inscribed with the names of more than 102,000
Australians who died in service to their country, it stares straight
down tree-lined Anzac Parade and across Lake Burley Griffin at
Parliament House, 4 km (2½ miles) distant. Built in the 1930s
and expanded often since, the museum/art gallery traces Aussie
military history from British colonial times through the World
War I tragedy of Gallipoli and the World War II attacks on Darwin to Australia's more modern involvement in the Vietnam
conflict. Free guided tours are available weekdays at 10:30 a.m.
and 1:30 p.m. Open daily 9:00 a.m. to 4:45 p.m. Free admission.

▲**Lake Burley Griffin**, the vivid blue centerpiece of Canberra, is highlighted by the Captain Cook Memorial Water Jet
(sending a column of water 430 feet above the lake from 10:00
a.m. to noon and again 2:00 to 4:00 p.m. daily) and the Carillon
(a 53-bell tower with free recitals on Wednesdays, Sundays, and
holidays). You can cruise the lake for an hour or two aboard the
City of Canberra or *Lady Claire* (leaving at noon and 1:00 p.m.
daily, cost A$6-$9), or rent a rowboat, canoe, paddle boat, or
windsurfer (A$7-$10 an hour). All water activities are centered
on West Basin in Acton Park.

Nightlife

Canberra's evening activity is pretty tame. **Juliana's**, in Noah's
Lakeside International Hotel on London Circuit, is the top dis-
cotheque; **Dorette's Bistro** is good for light classical and jazz.
Things liven up a bit on Friday and Saturday night, when several
small bars and taverns feature live entertainment for dancing.
Most residents find their diversions at RSL, leagues or other
clubs in Canberra or neighboring Queanbeyan, N.S.W. Visitors
are welcome; check out the **Canberra Labor Club**, Chandler

Street in Belconnen; the **Canberra Workers Club**, University Avenue and Children's Street, City; or the **Royals Rugby Union Football Club**, Weston Creek.

The modern **Canberra Theatre Centre** in Civic Square, off London Circuit, contains a theater, playhouse, gallery, restaurant, and rehearsal room. Everything from serious drama to world-class ballet to Gilbert and Sullivan to rock concerts is presented here. Call the box office (tel. 57-1077) for current offerings and prices.

CANBERRA TO BEECHWORTH

Today's route leads past the alpine resort of Thredbo in the Snowy Mountains via Corryong—reputed home of poet Banjo Paterson's "Man from Snowy River"—to Beechworth, a town straight out of the nineteenth-century gold rush era.

Suggested Schedule	
8:30	Leave Canberra, driving via Cooma to Thredbo.
11:30	Arrive at Thredbo. Take an hour for lunch and a look around, or buy some sandwich makings and stop for a picnic farther down the road.
2:30	After a drive down the Alpine Way through the Snowy Mountains, visit tiny Corryong.
4:30	Arrive in Yackandandah for a short tour of this village classified by the National Trust.
5:30	Reach Beechworth, whose main street has changed little in 100 years.

Today's Drive
Follow the signs off Canberra Avenue, southeast of Capitol Hill, to reach Route 23, the Monaro Highway. **Cooma**, 117 km (73 miles) south of Canberra, is about a 1½ -hour drive. Often considered the "gateway" to the Snowy Mountains because most skiers pass through it en route to the various resorts, this town of 8,000 also is headquarters of the Snowy Mountains Hydro-Electric Scheme, a massive project that created dams, power stations, and high-altitude lakes throughout the range west of here.
▲**Thredbo**, another 96 km (53 miles) of winding road west across the Snowy River, is built like a Tyrolean village with chalets dotting its alpine slopes. Regarded as Australia's No. 1 ski resort, it is also a popular summer escape with the country's highest golf course (1,370 meters or 4,495 feet), tennis courts, and horse-riding trails. Looming above the snowfields at the top of its Crackenback chair lift is Australia's highest peak, Mount Kosciusko, 2,229 meters (7,313 feet) in elevation. It's an easy walk for summer day-hikers and winter "langlaufers" (cross-country skiers). Nonskiers find spring the best time to visit, when the slopes are covered with wildflowers. Twenty separate lodges and a youth hostel provide beds and/or meals for skiers and other vacationers. The Thredbo Alpine Hotel, at the foot of the mountain, is a good choice for lunch with a view.

▲▲**Alpine Way** runs for 74 km (46 miles) through Kosciusko National Park from Thredbo to Khancoban. There is a A$5 admission fee to the park. More than half of the route is gravel, but it's well graded and is not normally (snow or heavy rain excepted) a difficult or dangerous drive. It's tremendously scenic, offering numerous vistas of the dense bush surrounding the headwaters of the Murray River, Australia's longest. On the off chance you've thrown a fishing pole in with your gear, the streams and lakes along this road are a good place to cast a line. Buy a license as you pass through Cooma (A$10 for 30 days).

Upon reaching **Khancoban**, a tiny township established for hydroelectric workers, you will have dropped nearly 3,500 feet from Thredbo. Follow the signs across the Murray River into the state of Victoria. It's 21 km (13 miles) to **Corryong**.

A broad main street establishes the character of this country center. Be sure to read "The Man from Snowy River" before you arrive. Jack Riley, generally regarded as the model for the poem, made his home in Corryong and is buried in the town cemetery. He and his legend are remembered at the **Man from Snowy River Folk Museum** with an eclectic but charming variety of exhibits. Located at the west end of town, it's open only from 2:00 to 3:00 p.m. Monday to Saturday. Admission is A$2.

Rather than backtracking on the Murray Valley Highway, proceed directly west about 120 km (75 miles) via Tallangatta to **Yackandandah**. (You can avoid the bottleneck of the Albury-Wodonga area by cutting over to the Kiewa Valley Highway near Tangambalanga.) So important is Yackandandah, historically and architecturally, that the entire township and surrounding hills are classified by the National Trust. Why the hills? Because the creeks and old gold diggings still yield alluvial gold to amateur prospectors. Take a few minutes to stroll the tree-lined avenues of town and photograph the buildings.

Beechworth

The most historically interesting town in northeast Victoria is Beechworth, 24 km (15 miles) southwest of Yackandandah. Established in 1839, it soon became one of Australia's richest goldfields, yielding 4.1 million ounces between 1852 and 1862. Commercial mining continued until 1920, and weekend panners still find gold in the creeks today.

By the time you arrive, the visitor information center in The Rock Cavern, at Ford and Camp streets, will probably be closed. You can take a "formal" self-guided tour tomorrow morning. For now, check into an accommodation with appropriate frontier atmosphere, dine, and get some shut-eye.

Sydney to Melbourne

1 INCH = 115 mi

Rose Cottage Bed and Breakfast, 42 Camp St. (tel. 057/28-1069), is a quaint four-bedroom home fully furnished with Victorian antiques. The price of A$40 single, A$60 double includes a full breakfast. Next door, the more commonplace but comfortable **Carriage Motor Inn**, 44 Camp St. (tel. 28-1830), charges A$36 single, A$42 double.

Transwell's Commercial Hotel, 30 Ford St. (tel. 28-1480), 118 years old, has toilets-down-the-hall rooms for A$25 single, A$35 double, including breakfast. (Superb dinners are priced from A$9.50 in the restaurant, and the pub serves A$6 counter meals.) **The Empire Hotel**, Camp and High streets (tel. 28-1030), has a similar setup with adequate rooms for A$20 single, A$40 double. Across the street from Transwell's, the **Youth Hostel** (tel. 28-1425) is housed in the old Star Hotel.

Aside from Transwell's, you can dine well over the counter at any of the town's four pubs. There's a Chinese restaurant, the **Chinese Village**, on Camp Street, and many travelers enjoy **Rosemary's Coffee Shop** on Ford Street.

BEECHWORTH TO MELBOURNE

After a morning tour of Beechworth, we'll visit the Brown Brothers Winery at Milawa and stop in at Glenrowan, where Ned Kelly—Australia's most notorious nineteenth-century bushranger—made his "last stand." The afternoon's highlight is the Sir Colin McKenzie Wildlife Sanctuary, an open-air reserve at Healesville that is the best of its kind in the world. Arrive in Melbourne in time for dinner.

Suggested Schedule

8:00	Breakfast in Beechworth, then explore the town and museum until about 10:30.
11:00	Tour Brown Brothers Winery and sample the product.
11:45	Dive into "Kelly Country" at the museums and roadside display in Glenrowan.
12:30	Grab picnic fixings in Benalla and enjoy them on the banks of Lake Nillahcootie.
3:00	Stroll for two hours among native Australian wildlife at the Sir Colin McKenzie Wildlife Sanctuary at Healesville.
6:30	Arrive in Melbourne. Check into your hotel and head for a well-earned dinner on Lygon Street.

Beechworth Sightseeing Highlights
No fewer than 32 of Beechworth's buildings have been classi-fied or recorded by the National Trust. The best place to start your exploration is the ▲▲**Burke Memorial Museum**, on Loch Street one-half block north of Camp Street. Established at this site in 1863, it is one of Australia's finest small-town museums. The collection is especially strong in pioneer history, the gold-rush era, and memorabilia of the local Chinese com-munity and the Kelly Gang. A new gallery reproduces a 16-shop main street of the mid-1800s with retail shops, a doctor's office, an assay office, a dance hall, and other establishments. Open 2:00 to 4:30 p.m. Monday, 11:00 a.m. to 4:30 p.m. Friday, 9:00 a.m. to 4:30 p.m. all other days. (For the sake of our tour, the Fri-day hours will hopefully be extended to 9:00 a.m. as well.) Admission is A$2.

On leaving the Burke Museum, pick up a copy of the lithographed brochure, "Beechworth Living History." Its map will direct you to 34 points of interest in the Beechworth area, most of them within easy walking distance. Among the properties administered by the National Trust are the **Carriage Museum**, behind Tanswell's Hotel, with an extensive collection of carriages and other turn-of-the-century vehicles, and the **Powder Magazine**, on Gorge Street at the west end of Camp Street, a fully restored brick building where gunpowder was cached for goldfield blasting in the 1850s. The Carriage Museum is open 10:00 a.m. to 12:30 p.m. and 1:30 to 4:30 p.m. daily from Boxing Day (Dec. 26) through May 31; other times, 1:30 to 4:30 p.m. The Powder Magazine is open daily from 10:00 a.m. to 12:30 p.m. and 1:30 to 4:30 p.m.; closed Good Friday and Christmas Day.

Other buildings of special interest include the **H.M. Training Prison**, the brewery museum in the old **M.B. Cellars**, and the **Chinese Burning Towers** at Beechworth Cemetery. If time allows, stop into the **Buckland Gallery**, perhaps the most interesting of several crafts shops in town.

The Route South

Milawa is little more than a crossroads on a secondary route midway between Beechworth and Glenrowan. But it's the site of one of Australia's finest wineries, the **Brown Brothers Vineyard and Winery**. John Francis Brown planted the first vines here in 1889, and four succeeding generations of Browns have carefully tended them. Sample some of the fermented grape juice—the cabernet and shiraz in red and the chardonnay and frontignac in white are particularly good—and take a bottle or two along for Melbourne's BYO restaurants.

▲**Glenrowan** is 21 km (13 miles) due west. Here, in 1880, an infamous 25-year-old outlaw named Ned Kelly and his three-man gang were cornered by police at the Glenrowan Inn. Kelly's companions, including his brother, were killed in a shootout; Ned himself was wounded and brought to trial in Melbourne, where he was hanged.

Over a period of fewer than three years before his capture, Kelly had cemented a reputation as a larcenous murderer. Yet his exploits—he was a superb horseman who wore a 97-pound hand-molded suit of armor to protect himself—so fascinated Australians of past and present that he has been immortalized in poems, plays, paintings, and even a movie starring Mick Jagger.

You can't miss Glenrowan's Kelly kitsch, even if you want to. A Paul Bunyanesque statue of Ned himself, garbed in his armor and toting a rifle, holds up a train emerging from a tunnel beside

Greater Melbourne

the Hume Highway. The so-called Glenrowan Tourist Centre contains the Ned Kelly Sound and Visual Museum, which has a fully animated gunfight half-hourly from 10:00 a.m. to 4:00 p.m. daily (admission A$8); next door is a re-creation of the cabin that Ned and his family called home; and everywhere you look there are Kelly T-shirts, books, records, cassette tapes, mugs, keychains, pennants, and everything else imaginable. I can only advise you to keep your pennies in your pocket when you stop.

If you stop for groceries another 24 km (15 miles) down the road at **Benalla**, famous for its rose gardens from late October through March, you can take your picnic basket to **Lake Nillah-cootie**, an oasis at the foot of Mount Samaria some 40 km (25 miles) south of town via the Midland Highway. After lunch, bypass Mansfield and pick up the Maroondah Highway, crossing the northern arm of serpentine Lake Eildon and continuing to charming Alexandra, the majestic Cathedral Range, and magnificent Maroondah fern forest. You'll arrive at the town of **Healesville** about 175 km (109 miles) from your picnic stop.

But don't stop in town. Follow the signs another 5 km southeast to the ▲▲▲ **Sir Colin McKenzie Wildlife Sanctuary**, often known simply as the "Healesville Sanctuary." This 79-acre reserve is home to nearly 2,000 mammals, birds, and reptiles of 200 species, all of them Australian natives. Few are behind bars, and visitors have the opportunity to stroll freely through kangaroo enclosures and parrot aviaries. You'll find everything from koalas to platypuses, wombats to Tasmanian devils, emus to lyrebirds. The sanctuary is open 9:00 a.m. to 5:00 p.m. every day of the year (arrive before 3:30 if you want to see the platypus); admission is reasonable at A$5.60. A restaurant and gift shop are on the grounds. I consider the sanctuary—established in 1921 in this natural bushland setting—to be Australia's best wildlife park. Others apparently agree, for it is the most visited attraction in the state of Victoria.

If you stay at the sanctuary until the closing hour, you'll avoid most of the rush-hour traffic (it will be coming toward you, instead of with you) as you drive the final 62 km (40 miles) west to Melbourne. Just stay on the Maroondah Highway all the way into the city.

Melbourne Orientation

A stately and sophisticated metropolis of 2.9 million people, Melbourne (pronounced "Melb'n," not "Mel-born") is Australia's second city. Its elegant Victorian buildings and large Mediterranean and Asian population combine to give it a cosmopolitan Old World atmosphere. It's no accident that Melbourne is the shopping, dining, entertainment, and sporting capital of the country.

Melbourne's role as Australia's financial center had more practical roots. Never a penal settlement, it was founded in 1835 by Europeans seeking to escape the more restrictive conditions on Tasmania. When the Victorian goldfields boomed in the 1850s, Melbourne became the center through which the riches were shipped. With their newfound wealth, Melbournians endowed their city with broad boulevards, beautiful parks, and classically handsome architecture. And although Sydney, with its superior harbor and 50-year head start, was the country's best-known city, it was Melbourne that became Australia's first national capital (1901-1927) and the host of its only Olympic Games (1956).

With a latitude of 38 degrees south, about the same distance from the equator as San Francisco is north, Melbourne has four distinct seasons—sometimes all in one day. Generalizations can be made—temperatures on summer days often range in the 80s Fahrenheit, while winter days average in the mid-50s—but the weather is definitely fickle, especially in the autumn months.

Melbourne's core is a neatly planned 1-by-2 km grid on the north bank of the Yarra River, with nine parallel streets running north-south and an equal number (five main streets and four widened alleys) crossing them from east to west. Swanston Street, which continues south across the Yarra, and Elizabeth Street, which connects to the Sydney-Canberra and Ballarat-Adelaide roads, are the main north-south thoroughfares. They are intersected by Flinders Street, flanking the river and the main metropolitan railway station; Collins Street, the address of most banks; Bourke Street, known for its shopping west of Swanston Street and its Chinatown east; Lonsdale Street, part of it called the Greek Precinct; and Latrobe Street, which extends east via Victoria Parade toward Healesville and the Dandenongs. You'll enter the city by this latter route.

City Transportation

The Metropolitan Transit System, known as the Met (tel. 617-0900), comprising rail and tram services, is Australia's best public transportation network. The trains stop at 235 stations within about a 40-km (25-mile) radius of the city center, and the web of electric trams (the only ones in Australia) fills in the gaps that the trains neglect. It seems as though you're never more than two blocks away from one. The system runs from 5:20 a.m. to 12:30 a.m. Monday to Saturday, 6:35 a.m. to 11:45 p.m. on Sunday. Single-ride tickets within the "Inner Neighborhood"—which includes almost all tourist attractions of note—are A75 cents; an unlimited travel two-hour ticket is A$1.80; and an all-day ticket is A$2.40. You can buy these and other tickets, as well as get free maps and more complete transit information, at Met depots, railway stations, and the Royal Arcade kiosk between Bourke and Little Collins streets.

A new and integral part of The Met is the Melbourne Underground Rail Loop, a A$400 million project linking five stations around the perimeter of the central city.

Melbourne's international and main domestic airport is at Tullamarine, 19 km (12 miles) northwest of the city center. It is served by taxis and by special buses with direct connections to downtown hotels.

Where to Stay

At the top of the line, Melbourne has two outstanding hotels that eschew modern steel and concrete for the classic look: **Menzies at Rialto**, 459 Collins St. (tel. 620-9111), and **The Windsor**, 103 Spring St. (tel. 653-0653). The Menzies has created an atrium out of two neo-Gothic nineteenth-century buildings, while The Windsor, opposite the old Parliament House, has retained its century-old feeling right down to the stained-glass dome lights in the dining room. Both cost A$245 and up.

In the moderate price bracket, the **Sheraton Hotel**, 13 Spring St. (tel. 63-9961), is centrally located opposite Treasury Gardens. On the north side, the **Downtowner Motel**, 66 Lygon St., Carlton (tel. 663-5555), is close to Melbourne's best

Downtown Melbourne

TO ADELAIDE, BALLARAT & AIRPORT — TO CANBERRA & SYDNEY
GRATTAN — Melbourne University — LYGON
QUEENSBURY — Restaurants
VICTORIA
Downtowner Motel
Carlton Gardens
Old Melbourne Gaol
LA TROBE
ELIZABETH SWANSTON
Museum
LITTLE GREECE
LONSDALE
CHINATOWN
BOURKE — General Post Office
Spencer St. Station   (mall)
The Windsor • Parliament
Hotel Australia •• Tourism Commission
COLLINS
Menzies Rialto Hotel   Hyatt on Collins
FLINDERS   Treasury Gardens   Fitzroy Gardens
• World Trade Centre   YARRA   Flinders St. Station
                    RIVER
Arts Centre •
Night Clubs
National Gallery
                                    Melbourne Cricket Ground
CLARENDON   KINGS WAY   ST. KILDA   SWAN   BATMAN   Richmond Cricket Grnd
TO PRINCES HWY.   • Shrine of Remembrance   Olympic Park

restaurant strip. A double is A$100. The **Albert Heights Apartments**, 83 Albert St., East Melbourne (tel. 419-0955), have one-bedroom kitchen suites for about A$80, with AAA discounts. About 4 km south of the city center but on the tram line are the **President Melbourne**, 63 Queens Road (tel. 529-4300), and the **Crest International**, 47 Barkly St., St. Kilda (tel. 537-1788).

In the economy class, try the **Victoria Hotel**, 215 Little Collins St. (tel. 653-0441), downtown, or the charming **Magnolia Court**, 101 Powlett St., East Melbourne (tel. 419-4222), facing

Fitzroy Gardens. For budget lodging, the city's two **YHA youth hostels** are within a block of each other in North Melbourne, 3 km from downtown. The larger of the two, 76 Chapman St. (tel. 328-3595), charges A$13 a head for its 50 double rooms. The older dormitory-style hostel at 50 Abbotsford St. (tel. 328-2880) charges A$12. You can also find good accommodations year-round at the University of Melbourne's **International House**, 241 Royal Parade, Parkville (tel. 347-2351), about 4 km north of downtown, with single rooms and shared baths.

Where to Eat
Melbourne is an epicure's delight, a city with a multitude of excellent restaurants to appeal to any palate. . .and any wallet. This is partly a response to its attitude of self-importance but perhaps even more a result of its broad base of ethnic diversity. The Greeks (only Athens and Thessalonika have larger Greek populations than Melbourne), Italians, Yugoslavs, Turks, Lebanese, Chinese, and Vietnamese, in particular, have left their marks on Melbourne's dining habits.

There are several restaurant "strips" in Melbourne but perhaps none so acclaimed as Lygon Street in Carlton, a short stroll up Russell Street from the city center. The main Italian neighborhood of Melbourne, this is the place for pasta and pizzas. **Toto's** (No. 101), **El Gambero** (No. 215), **Il Gusto** (No. 256), and **Tiamo's** (No. 303) are among the best known, all serving good meals for less than A$10 per person. But this district is no longer strictly Italian; check the side streets for Japanese food at the **Samurai**, 210 Drummond St.; Mexican at **Cha Chi's**, 161 Nicholson St.; Malay and Chinese at the **Bali House**, 157 Elgin St.; vegetarian at **Shakahari**, 329 Lygon St.

Melbourne's most famous restaurant, **Mietta's**, is downtown near the deluxe international hotels—at 7 Alfred Place (between Exhibition and Russell streets off Collins Street). Put out A$100 for two, and you'll get an exquisite continental dinner with equally generous service. But you can eat well in the city center without breaking your budget. You can't go wrong in Chinatown (Little Bourke Street east of Swanston) if you check out the menus in the windows and see where the locals are eating. I like the **Bamboo House**, 47 Little Bourke St., for Mandarin cuisine and the **Empress of China**, 120 Little Bourke St., for Cantonese.

The Greek restaurants on Lonsdale Street east of Swanston are also excellent. Try **Stalactites** (open 24 hours) at Lonsdale and Russell streets. You'll find even more Greek eateries—plus a slew of Vietnamese places—in the Richmond district east of the city center. Similarly, there's a Turkish dining strip on Sydney Road in Brunswick, north of downtown.

A personal favorite for a splurge is **Percy's**, 384 Punt Road, South Yarra, an innovative BYO spot with a blackboard menu that changes daily. Other local choices include **Cafe Lisboa** (Portuguese), 413 Brunswick St., Fitzroy; **Costa Brava** (Spanish), 36 Johnston St., Fitzroy; and **Isabella's**, a bistro at Russell and Little Collins streets downtown.

For lunch, **Jimmy Watson's Wine Bar**, 333 Lygon St., is hard to beat for good, cheap cuisine in an amiable atmosphere. On the south side, the **Station Hotel**, Chapel and Peel streets in Prahran, has counter meals for as little as A$3.

With some 2,000 restaurants in Melbourne, there's never a fear about where to eat. So sophisticated is the city in its dining habits that there's a white-linen restaurant aboard a tram and another on a double-decker bus!

Helpful Hints

The **Victorian Tourism Center** (tel. 619-9444), known as "Victour," handles tourist information on Melbourne city as well as Victoria. It is centrally located at 230 Collins St. and is open 9:00 a.m. to 5:00 p.m. Monday to Friday, 9:00 a.m. to noon Saturday. There is also a **Melbourne Tourism Authority** (tel. 654-2288) on the 20th floor of Nauru House, 80 Collins St.

The **General Post Office**, at the corner of Bourke and Elizabeth streets, is open 8:00 a.m. to 6:00 p.m. Monday to Friday. Most city banks are open 9:30 a.m. to 4:00 p.m. Monday to Thursday, 9:30 a.m. to 5:00 p.m. Friday. Shop hours vary, but you can generally expect downtown merchants to be open from 9:00 a.m. to 5:30 p.m. Monday to Thursday, 9:00 a.m. to 9:00 p.m. Friday, 9:00 a.m. to noon Saturday.

There's an **American Consulate** in South Melbourne at 24 Albert Road (tel. 697-7900) and a **Canadian Consulate** downtown at 151 Flinders St. (tel. 654-1433).

In case of emergencies, dial 000.

MELBOURNE

Explore the city today. Wander through ethnic neighborhoods,
sophisticated shopping arcades, the highbrow banking district.
The Old Gaol and the National Museum of Victoria are worthy
stops. Don't miss the beautiful Victorian Arts Centre or the
nation's best botanic gardens. But don't overdo the sightseeing.
Here in sports-crazy Melbourne, try to soak up some local culture by attending (depending on the season) a "footie" (Australian rules football) match, cricket test, or horse race.

Suggested Schedule

9:00	A good way to see Melbourne is to start at the north end of downtown and work your way south on Swanston Street. First stop is Victoria Market, where rows of fresh fruit vendors can supply a juicy breakfast.
10:00	The Old Melbourne Gaol and Penal Museum.
10:45	The National Museum of Victoria, last resting place of Phar Lap.
11:45	Explore the Greek Precinct and Chinatown, stopping in one or the other for lunch.
1:00	Bourke Street Mall and shopping arcades.
2:00	Collins Street, Melbourne's true "Golden Mile."
2:30	Victorian Arts Centre, the largest multiarts complex in the world.
3:30	The National Gallery of Victoria, Australia's finest art museum.
5:00	Royal Botanic Gardens.
6:00	Dinner.
7:00	Join the fanatic throngs at a sports event. There's always something going on Saturday night.
10:00	Climax your day with a little nightlife.

Sightseeing Highlights
▲**Victoria Market** is a large, open-air market near the intersection of Queen and Victoria streets. (The main entrance is off
Franklin Street.) On Tuesday, Friday and Saturday mornings
starting at 6:00 a.m., it's a multicultural potpourri of fruit and
vegetable vendors, while on Sundays from 9:00 a.m. to 4:00

p.m., it turns into an enormous flea market especially popular among craft and antique dealers.

▲▲The Old Melbourne Gaol and Penal Museum, Russell Street near Lygon, is a dank and morbid but fascinating relic of the days (1841 to 1929) when men were men and felons were hanged. Here are the gallows and isolation cells known and feared by hundreds of convicts, including the notorious bushranger Ned Kelly. The jail exhibits Kelly's handmade armor and his "death mask," created for phrenologists to study possible clues to his deviant behavior. Open 10:00 a.m. to 5:00 p.m. daily except Sunday. Admission A$3.50.

▲▲The National Museum of Victoria, Swanston and LaTrobe streets, has an excellent exhibit of state history, a new science and technology section, plus good natural history and ethnography displays. Deep within its chambers, however, is the reason so many Australians consider this a religious site. Phar Lap, generally regarded as the greatest racehorse that ever lived, stands within a glass display case—at least, his stuffed skin does. (His heart is in Canberra.) The steed won an incredible 37 of his 51 starts, earning over A$133,000 before dying a mysterious death in Menlo Park, California, in 1932 at the age of 5½. (If you saw the 1983 Australian movie, you know all this.) The museum is open daily from 10:00 a.m. to 5:00 p.m. Free admission.

The Greek Precinct of Lonsdale Street, from Swanston to Russell Street, is being upgraded to emphasize the outdoor cafés and colorful specialty shops. The traditional Edwardian character of the buildings has been maintained. If you're here in March or April, chances are you'll catch a festival.

▲Chinatown—two blocks from Swanston Street to Exhibition Street, bisected by Little Bourke Street—is linked to the Greek Precinct via Heffernan Lane. Chinese have lived in this neighborhood since 1854. The opium dens have long since closed, but many of the butchers, bakers, and candlemakers still ply trades learned from their forefathers. Today, the restaurants and shops on Little Bourke and its side lanes, especially Celestial Avenue, comprise the most interesting Chinatown in the Southern Hemisphere. The Museum of Chinese Australian History, 22 Cohen Place, contains photographs, artifacts, and an audiovisual presentation. Open weekdays except Friday 10:00 a.m. to 4:30 p.m., weekends noon to 4:30 p.m.

▲Bourke Street Mall is the shopping center of Australia's shopping capital. The Myer Emporium, for example, is the world's second largest department store (after Marshall Field's in Chicago), taking up a good portion of two city blocks on the north side of the mall. Next door to it is David Jones, Australia's answer to J.C. Penney. The south side of the mall is interlaced by a maze of delightfully restored shopping arcades. In particular, check out the Royal Arcade, with its campy 1892 clock depicting Gog and Magog striking the time.

There are several other great shopping streets in the suburbs. Armadale High Street is packed with antique, craft, book, and clothing shops; Chapel Street and Toorak Road are the hubs of a glitzy high-fashion neighborhood in South Yarra; and St. Kilda's Acland Street is famous for its pastry shops.

Parliament House, on Spring Street at the east end of Bourke, was built in 1856 and served as the federal Parliament until the provisional house in Canberra opened in 1927. It still serves as Victoria's state assembly chambers. Guided tours are offered at 10:00 a.m., 11:00 a.m., 2:00 p.m., and 3:00 p.m. Monday through Friday.

▲**Collins Street** is where the nation's most important financial institutions are housed, many of them in Victorian gold-rush masterpieces spliced between steel-and-glass skyscrapers. If you're here on a weekday, take a walking tour, starting at the ANZ Banking Museum (open 9:30 a.m. to 4:00 p.m. Monday to Friday) in the basement of the Australia-New Zealand Bank, 386 Collins St. Then step inside the institution upstairs for a look-around, and also have a peek into the Bank of New Zealand (No. 395), National Australian Bank (No. 335), and Westpac (No. 331). The Melbourne Stock Exchange, 351 Collins St., has a third floor visitors gallery with a broad view of the trading floor. It's open Monday to Friday from 10:00 a.m. to 12:15 p.m. and 2:00 to 3:15 p.m.

▲▲**The Victorian Arts Centre** is modern Melbourne's pride and joy. The city proudly trumpets that this is "the largest arts center in the world." Indeed, the complex—completed in 1985—includes a 2,600-seat concert hall, three theaters for opera, ballet, and drama, three licensed restaurants, an art shop, a museum, and the adjoining National Gallery of Victoria. Its 500-foot Eiffel-like spire, which towers over the Yarra River beside St. Kilda Road, can be seen for miles around.

A variety of tours are offered to show off the Centre and its unusual architecture. There are morning tea tours weekdays for A$14, or luncheon tours for A$36. Evening tours, starting promptly at 5:00 p.m. Monday to Friday, include dinner and a show for A$57. Short tours at 10:30 a.m. daily cost A$2.75; Sunday backstage tours are A$6.

The Melbourne Symphony Orchestra often plays free lunchtime concerts, and every Friday from 5:00 to 7:00 p.m., there's a free jazz show in the basement Monsanto Lounge. Bookings should be made for all other performances and tours by calling 617-8211.

▲**The Performing Arts Museum** in the concert hall is highly regarded internationally. Its changing exhibits range from silent films or horror movies to re-creations of Dame Nellie Melba's operatic recordings. Open 11:00 a.m. to 5:00 p.m. Monday to Friday, noon to 5:00 p.m. weekends. Admission A$2.40.

▲▲▲**The National Gallery of Victoria**, on the south side of the Victorian Arts Centre at 180 St. Kilda Road, was Australia's first public art gallery (founded in 1861) and is still the finest in the Southern Hemisphere. Its most popular galleries to overseas visitors are those of Aboriginal and Oceanic art and of Australian art, especially featuring its noted Heidelberg school of late nineteenth-century impressionists—Tom Roberts, Arthur Streeton, Frederick McCubbin, and Charles Condon. Its collection of more than 50,000 works also includes divisions of European, British, and American art, Asian art, pre-Columbian art, costumes and textiles, decorative arts, prints and drawings, and photography. Open daily except Monday from 10:00 a.m. to 5:00 p.m. Admission A$1.20.

▲▲**The Royal Botanic Gardens**, a half-kilometer stroll south and east of the Arts Centre, is considered one of the world's best landscaped gardens. More than 12,000 plant species thrive in the 88 acres of lawns, garden beds, and ornamental lakes, along with over 50 species of birds.

Adjacent to the gardens is the much larger **King's Domain**, containing the massive Shrine of Remembrance war memorial; the circa-1840 LaTrobe's Cottage, Victoria's original government house (open daily 11:00 a.m. to 4:30 p.m., admission A$2.40); and the Sidney Myer Music Bowl, an outdoor amphitheater in summer, a covered public ice rink in winter. The 11-km Yarra River Bikeway starts here; bicycles can be hired opposite the Botanic Gardens in Alexandra Avenue from 11:00 a.m. to dusk weekends and holidays.

Melbourne's other famous parks include **Fitzroy Gardens**, in East Melbourne between Wellington Parade and Albert Street. Its highlight is Captain Cook's Cottage, transported here from Yorkshire, England, in 1934 and reassembled (open 9:00 a.m. to 5:00 p.m. daily, admission A$1.30). The adjacent **Treasury Gardens**, facing Spring Street, contain a John Kennedy memorial. **Carlton Gardens**, Victoria Street opposite Spring, contains the Royal Exhibition Buildings built in 1880 for the inauguration of the commonwealth of Australia. **Albert Park**, between South Melbourne and St. Kilda, has a large lake with boat rentals.

▲**The Royal Melbourne Zoo**, on Elliott Avenue in Royal Park (north of the city center), is the third oldest zoo on Earth. The aviary, they say, is bigger than Paris' Cathedral of Notre Dame. The 55 acres have recently been relandscaped, with most of the

336 species now in simulated natural environments. Open 9:00 a.m. to 5:30 p.m. daily. Admission A$5.60.

▲**Como House** (1855), on Como Avenue in South Yarra, and ▲**Ripponlea** (1887), on Hotham Street in Elsternwick, are two beautiful colonial mansions set in spacious suburban gardens. Both have been refurnished with the trappings of the Victorian elite; both are open daily 10:00 a.m. to 5:00 p.m. and charge A$4 admission. (Ripponlea has limited winter hours.)

▲**The Polly Woodside**, anchored in the Yarra River at Normanby Road and Phayer Street in South Melbourne, is a restored iron-hulled Irish sailing vessel now finding new duty as the focus of a maritime museum. Open Monday to Friday 10:00 a.m. to 4:00 p.m., weekends noon to 5:00 p.m. Admission A$5.

The City Explorer Bus (tel. 650-1511) leaves the Flinders Street Station hourly from 10:00 a.m. to 4:00 p.m. every day but Monday. It stops at Captain Cook's Cottage, the Old Gaol, the National Museum, the Polly Woodside, and the National Gallery. One-day tickets for the on-again, off-again loop are A$10.

Sports in Melbourne

Australia in general—and Melbourne in particular—comes to a stop on the first Tuesday of November when the Melbourne Cup is run at Flemington Racecourse. In fact, this world-famous horse race is celebrated as a public holiday in Victoria. And that's indicative of the reverence with which Melbournians regard sports in general.

After all, this is where Australian rules football was invented. Victorians have set out to evangelize the world with this sport that isn't soccer, isn't rugby, certainly isn't American football, but has elements of all three—and some of its own. Most of Australia's capital cities are now represented in the Victorian Football League, and the ESPN cable television network in the United States broadcasts a game of the week. Upwards of 100,000 fans attend major matches at the venerable Melbourne Cricket Ground. The season starts in April and concludes with the Grand Final on the last Saturday of September.

About the time "footie" is winding down, cricket is just beginning. Its season runs from October to March, concluding with the Sheffield Shield, pitting each Australian state against the others until one claims the national championship. A single test match can take five 8-hour days to play.

Melbourne hosts many other important sports events, including a major international tennis tournament. To find out what's happening (and where) during your visit, check the sports page of *The Age*, Australia's best newspaper.

Melbourne Nightlife
Melbourne doesn't have any equivalent to Sydney's Kings Cross.
Its nightlife is spread across the metropolis, from downtown to
the suburbs. St. Kilda, a short hop south of the city center, tends
to be the hippest area; Richmond (east) and Carlton (north) can
also be lively.

The Friday morning edition of *The Age* gives full listings of
the entertainment week ahead. Rock music dominates the
scene, but you'll find far more jazz and acoustic music in Melbourne than in other big cities.

The only thing approaching a downtown "strip" is King Street
from Collins to Flinders. In one block, there's live rock at **Inflation** and the **Melbourne Underground**; discos at the **Hippo-
drome** and the **York Butter Factory**; cabaret at **Lazzars
International**; jazz and folk at the **Grainstore Tavern**. Some
of the nightspots are open all night—you can rage 'til 7:00 a.m.

The **Limerick Arms Hotel** in South Melbourne and the
Bridge Hotel in Richmond are two of the city's best venues for
live jazz, while the **Moomba Hotel** in North Melbourne is good
for country sounds Wednesday through Friday.

The No. 1 meeting spot in town, at this writing, was the new
Hyatt on Collins, at the corner of Russell Street. The casual
bars and restaurants in the basement of its atrium are packed
from the off-work hours to closing. **Zanie's**, a trendy bar-bistro
at Lonsdale and Russell streets, draws a good crowd. The **Sher-
lock Holmes Inn**, 421 Collins St., attracts lovers of traditional
British pubs.

Young and Jackson's, 1 Swanston St. at Flinders, is Melbourne's most famous pub and one of its oldest. Since the Melbourne Exhibition of 1880, it has displayed above its bar an oil
painting of "Chloe"—a full-length nude that once shocked Victorian sentiments.

For symphony, theater, opera, and ballet, the obvious first
choice is the **Victorian Arts Centre** (see "Sightseeing Highlights"). Other major stages downtown—**Her Majesty's Theatre**, 219 Exhibition St., and the **Princess Theatre**, 163 Spring
St.—are within three blocks of each other. This section of
downtown Melbourne, along Bourke Street between Spring and
Swanston, is also the location of most cinema houses for first-
run movies.

Melbourne hosts two major festivals during the year.
Moomba, in March, is the Mardi Gras Down Under. Gian Carlo
Menotti's Spoleto Arts Festival, in September/October, is a more
sedate but culturally fulfilling event.

BALLARAT

Ballarat is synonymous with two subjects near and dear to Australians' hearts: gold and independence. Today's outing covers both ends of this historic Victorian city—Sovereign Hill, the country's No. 1 theme park, faithful to its 1850s heyday; and the Eureka Stockade, site (in 1854) of a much-heralded rebellion unique in Australian history.

Suggested Schedule

8:00	Leave Melbourne, heading west on the Great Western Freeway (Highway 8).
10:00	Arrive in Ballarat. Sovereign Hill is the town's central attraction. Plan to spend several hours, including lunch.
2:00	Cross the street to the Gold Museum.
3:00	Relive the glory of the Eureka Stockade.
4:00	See Montrose Cottage, the Botanic Gardens, or another of Ballarat's attractions.
5:30	Head back to Melbourne for dinner and rest.

Ballarat Orientation

Victoria's second-largest city (pop. 90,000), Ballarat is located 113 km (70 miles) west of Melbourne. It was founded by gold diggers in 1851 and quickly became an Eldorado, with fortune hunters from around the world converging on the settlement after hearing fairy tales about gold nuggets being plucked off the streets. In fact, the argonauts had to work for their gold, but they pulled an estimated 20 million ounces from the hills before the last mine closed in 1918. At today's prices, that would be worth about US$9.4 billion.

Much of the money that gold wrought was poured into constructing a beautiful town on the frontier. With the opening of the railroad in 1962, Ballarat became the gateway to western Victoria, and its future was assured. Today, it is known for its gardens and art galleries as much as for its historic sites. The Western Highway—Stuart Street through most of downtown—bisects Ballarat into northern and southern halves. The Gold Centre Tourist Centre (tel. 053/32-2694), on Lydiard Street outside the railway station, is two blocks north of the highway near the business center of town. Sovereign Hill is perhaps a mile south of the center on Bradshaw Street (just off Main Road). The

Eureka Stockade, exhibition, and diorama are on Stawell Street, just south of the Western Highway at the east end of Ballarat.

City Transportation
If you don't drive to Ballarat—if you perchance took the train or bus from Melbourne—you can shuttle to the town's attractions on the Shuttlebus (tel. 361-815). Seven loop trips a day are operated around the city, taking in Sovereign Hill and the Eureka Stockade. You can board at the Tourism Centre at the railway station, disembark, and reboard wherever you choose along the route for A$8. The Shuttlebus also travels between Ballarat and Melbourne's Tullamarine Airport three or four times daily, with A$38 covering round-trip transportation plus admission charges at Sovereign Hill and the Eureka Exhibition.

Sightseeing Highlights
▲▲▲ **Sovereign Hill** is a place of living history, an authentic re-creation of Australia's most important gold-mining township of the 1850s. Operated by a nonprofit local association whose 200 volunteers dress in period costume, the park has three main sections. In the Red Hill Gully Diggings (faithful to the period 1851-1855), brightly dressed miners emerge from their tents and mud huts to show visitors how to pan for alluvial gold. In the Goldmining Township (1854-1861), horse-drawn coaches roll past 29 separate working businesses—among them a blacksmith, coachbuilder, tinsmith, confectioner, printer, potter, and furniture maker with a steam-driven lathe. In the Mining Museum (1860-1918), you can travel underground to learn how quartz reef mining was done, while above you a thunderous stamper battery crushes the gold-bearing quartz.

Main Street is Sovereign Hill's core. You can dine in style at the New York Bakery or the licensed United States Hotel. (Takeaway food and barbecue supplies are also available in the Township.) You can attend comedy sketches in the Victoria Theatre, or try your hand at skittles in the Empire Bowling Saloon.

Low-cost accommodations are available at Government Camp, a re-created 1850s military barracks on a hill overlooking the Township. Though the buildings might appear old, they're comfortably modern within. Families of four can stay for A$49 a night (for four); there's also a YHA youth hostel on the site. The park is open daily (except Christmas) from 9:30 a.m. to 5:00 p.m. Admission is A$11.50; for A$34, you can get a Gold Pass, which includes a coach ride and admission to the adjacent Gold Museum.

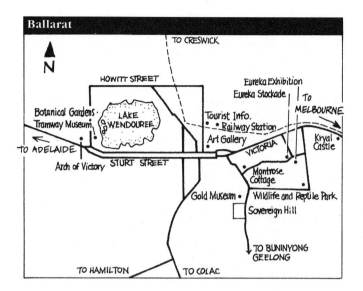

▲▲The Gold Museum, on Bradshaw Street across from the Sovereign Hill car park, is a worthy adjunct to the theme park. Its historical exhibits, while emphasizing the gold-rush era and Eureka Stockade rebellion, also recall central Victoria's Aboriginal history and the creation of its wool industry. The Gold Pavilion displays important private collections of rare gold coins from around the world and turn-of-the-century Chinese artifacts. Open 9:30 a.m. to 5:30 p.m. daily except Christmas. Admission A$2.

▲▲Eureka Stockade is a name with the same ring to Australians as the Alamo has to Texans. Like Davy Crockett and Jim Bowie et al., the miners lost this battle—but they won the war.

Mercilessly taxed and oppressed by the British colonial administration, the diggers made a gallant stand for their democratic rights. The climax came on December 3, 1854, when government troopers attacked a stockaded position held by miners near the Eureka diggings. Six troopers and 22 miners died. The tragedy shocked Victoria's colonial leaders into introducing long-awaited reforms in the goldfields. Within a year, two leaders of the revolt were elected to the first Victorian Parliament under a new constitution.

Today, at the Eureka Street Parklands (at the corner of Stawell Street), the rebellion is remembered by a memorial, a reconstructed stockade, and a diorama of the incident. More impressive is the Eureka Exhibition, catty-corner from the memorial at

Eureka and Kline streets, with a series of computer-controlled scenes depicting various episodes of the revolt. Open daily 9:00 a.m. to 6:00 p.m.

The miners' famous Southern Cross banner flew over the stockade for only five days—yet Aussies hold it in the same esteem as Americans do Betsy Ross's "13 stars on a field of blue." The Eureka flag can be seen in the Ballarat Fine Art Gallery, 40 Lydiard St. (near the Tourism Centre).

▲**Montrose Cottage**, 111 Eureka St., is the last original bluestone masonry cottage surviving from 1850s Ballarat. Classified by the National Trust, it contains the small Eureka Museum of Social History. Open daily 9:30 a.m. to 5:00 p.m.

The 100-acre **Botanic Gardens** encompass Lake Wendouree on the northwest side of Ballarat. Prime Ministers Avenue, within the gardens, is flanked by bronze busts of all Australian prime ministers, right up through the leader in 1989, Bob Hawke.

Kryal Castle, 8 km east of Ballarat on the Western Highway, is a curiosity: a re-created medieval castle where costumed actors reenact the life and pageantry of the Middle Ages. There's jousting, sword-fighting, even the occasional hanging, and a tavern where a medieval banquet is held every Saturday night. Open 9:30 a.m. to 5:00 p.m. daily except Christmas.

Golda's World of Dolls, 148 Eureka St., displays more than 2,000 rare antique and period-costumed dolls from all over the world. Open 1:00 to 5:00 p.m. daily except Fridays.

The Arch of Victory at the west end of Ballarat marks the beginning of the tree-lined, 21-km-long Avenue of Honour dedicated to the men and women of Ballarat who volunteered for active service abroad during World War I.

DANDENONG RANGES AND PHILLIP ISLAND

The "Blue Dandenongs," a relaxing day trip on the east side of Melbourne, contain many beautiful gardens, a unique sculpture forest, a park noted for its lyrebirds, and various other attractions. The day's highlight comes at dusk, when hundreds or thousands of tiny fairy penguins parade from the sea to their burrows up a concrete walkway, as hundreds of cameras click away.

Suggested Schedule

9:00	Leave Melbourne as soon as rush hour has ended.
10:15	Stroll through the William Ricketts Sanctuary, with its environmentally oriented sculptures of Aboriginal Mother Nature theme.
11:00	Visit Mount Dandenong Observatory to gaze at the high-rises of Melbourne in the distance.
11:30	The pretty artisans' village of Olinda is also the site of the National Rhododendron Gardens.
12:15	Lunchtime at a tearoom in Olinda or Sassafras.
1:00	The elusive lyrebird runs free in Sherbrooke Forest Park.
2:00	Take a quick swim at Emerald Lake Park or visit a model railway museum near the terminus of the Puffing Billy steam train from Belgrave.
4:30	Arrive at Phillip Island for the penguin parade. The parade occurs about dusk, so the exact time varies from season to season.
After Dark	Return to Melbourne, stopping for dinner en route.

(Note: on Sundays, these roads are always packed by local day-trippers. Plan to skip a couple of attractions in the Dandenongs to reach Phillip Island on time.)

The Dandenong Ranges

The forested mountains east of Melbourne aren't especially high—Mount Dandenong itself is only 633 meters (2,076 feet)—but that's enough to lift them above the occasional smog of Port Phillip Bay and endow them with a rich plant and animal life. A surprising number of artists and nature lovers choose to live in the Dandenongs and commute 60 to 90 minutes (each way) to the city daily.

The fastest route to the Dandenong Ranges is to head back east on the Maroondah Highway as though going to Healesville, but turn right at Ringwood on the well-marked Mount Dandenong Road. A drive of about an hour from the city brings you to Montrose at the northern end of the Mount Dandenong Tourist Road. Sightseeing highlights of the Dandenongs, moving down the road from north to south, include:

▲▲**William Ricketts Sanctuary**. Like J.R.R. Tolkien gone mad, Ricketts—who celebrated his 90th birthday in 1989—is an eccentric musician-turned-artist-turned environmental radical. His enchanting clay sculptures decorate a lovely fern forest on the slopes of Mount Dandenong; indeed, they are a part of the forest, carefully melded to existing trees, rocks, and brooks. All of Ricketts' work has Aboriginal and spiritual overtones. His more recent sculptures also make fierce animal rights and antiexploitation statements. "Being part of nature," he writes, "we are brothers to the birds and trees. Will you then join with us in the sacredness of beauty?" Open 10:00 a.m. to 4:30 p.m. daily. Admission A$3.

▲**Mount Dandenong Observatory**. Outside the mountain-top restaurant and tearoom are a roadside observation area and a handful of coin-in-the-slot telescopes to gaze across at the metropolis of Melbourne in the near west.

Edward Henty Cottage. A pioneer museum and antique shop occupy the former home of one of the Dandenongs' early residents. Located a short distance above Olinda. Admission to the museum is A$1.50.

▲**Olinda**. Art galleries and small restaurants specializing in midday Devonshire teas line the road around this picturesque village. It's worth getting out of the car and walking around.

▲**National Rhododendron Gardens**. Rhody lovers go bananas over these Olinda gardens in the spring and summer. By autumn, there's not much to look at. Admission A$3.50.

▲**Sherbrooke Forest Park**. Take any of the tranquil trails through this lush nature preserve and you're likely to see or hear the lyrebird, a grouse-sized ground bird with a long, lacy, peacocklike tail used in courtship demonstrations. The lyrebird is remarkable for its ability to mimic almost any sound it hears, from other birds to machinery. (I was once awakened while camping by the sound of a logging truck. There were no logging roads nearby, but there were lyrebirds.) Also in the forest are Sherbrooke Falls, Alfred Nicholas Memorial Gardens, and four picnic grounds with barbecue facilities.

Fern Tree Gully National Park. Just above the town of Upper Ferntree Gully, this small park encompassing a valley of beautiful fern trees offers pleasant walks and colorful rosellas galore.
Belgrave. Another artists' community, somewhat larger than Olinda, Belgrave lies at a major junction in the Dandenongs. It's best known as the depot for Puffing Billy.
▲▲**Puffing Billy**. Australia's best-known narrow-gauge steam railroad—built in 1900 to carry farm produce—packs its wooden cars with weekend and holiday day-trippers year-round, daily during school vacations (except on days of total fire ban). Puffing Billy typically leaves Belgrave at 10:30 a.m. on its 13-km (8-mile), 40-minute run up and down the ridges to Emerald Lake Park, returning at 12:40 p.m. There are additional runs on weekends. Round-trip fare is A$9.70 for adults, A$6.50 for kids. (Call 870-8411 for timetable specifics.) There's a Steam Museum at Menzies Creek, open 11:00 a.m. to 5:00 p.m. Sundays and holidays, with a collection of early locomotives. We won't have time for a ride on Puffing Billy on this itinerary, but you may enjoy it if you have an extra day or two in Melbourne.
▲**Emerald Lake Park**. A spacious, well-kept park surrounding a lake popular with swimmers and fishermen, this is the eastern terminus of Puffing Billy. Above the station is a pavilion containing Australia's largest model railway: over 2 kilometers of track. A youth hostel stands near the park's entrance. In Emerald village are many quaint shops and craft galleries.

Phillip Island

It will take about 30 minutes to drive from Emerald Lake Park to Pakenham and another 90 minutes to follow the South Gippsland and Bass highways south to San Remo, at the east end of the 604-meter (2,100-foot) Narrows Bridge connecting Phillip Island to the Victorian mainland.

Phillip Island's main attraction—one of the outstanding sights in all of Australia—is the ▲▲▲**Penguin Parade** at Summerland Beach, near the island's southwestern tip, every night of the year. A colony of fairy penguins numbering in the thousands spend most of their days fishing in Bass Strait, returning at dusk to their burrows in the sand dunes at this protected reserve. Bright lights illuminate the beach as the penguins straggle in to land and up a concrete walkway, while a crowd of camera-happy tourists quietly view from controlled areas behind a wire fence. These little (foot-high) birds are so cuddly looking that it's hard not to smile as you watch them waddle through their nightly ritual, apparently oblivious to all the human attention.

You can buy tickets to the viewing area (for A$3.50) at the Penguin Reserve office beginning 30 minutes before the parade, or at the Phillip Island Information Centre near San Remo, open daily 9:00 a.m. to 5:00 p.m. Flash cameras are not permitted.

The penguins aren't the only wild denizens of 25,000-acre Phillip Island. Koalas roam freely in the eucalyptus groves of **Oswin Roberts Reserve**. Fur seals maintain an offshore colony on **The Nobbies**, a 50-million-year-old volcanic rock stack: up to 4,500 of the marine mammals breed here in November and December. Mutton birds (short-tailed shearwaters) nest on Cape Woolamai, the island's southeasternmost point.

Len Lukey Memorial Museum and Gardens, on Back Beach Road in Cowes, exhibits a good collection of vintage cars and racing vehicles from a late-lamented motor racing track. The island also features dairy and shell museums, a center for wool artisans, three chicory kilns, a historic homestead on Churchill Island (connected to Phillip Island by a footbridge at Newhaven), a small zoo, a large blowhole, a cavern, golf courses, and other standard resort amenities.

Cowes, the island's main town (on the north shore), has ample accommodation and eating places. (In summer, it's best to dine before the parade, because the restaurants close early.)

ALICE SPRINGS

Drop your car at Melbourne's Tullamarine Airport and catch a morning flight to Alice Springs. You'll have all afternoon and evening to explore this outback oasis. Visit the Old Telegraph Station and the Royal Flying Doctor Service. To climax your day, ride a camel down the dry Todd River bed to dinner at a desert winery.

Suggested Schedule	
6:30	Return car to Tullamarine Airport.
7:25	Depart Melbourne on Ansett Flight 200 for Alice Springs.
10:40	Arrive at Alice Springs.
11:30	Check into your accommodations.
1:00	Orient yourself at the Anzac Hill viewpoint.
1:30	See the Old Telegraph Station.
2:30	Visit the School of the Air.
3:00	Drop in on the Royal Flying Doctor Service.
4:00	Take a camel to dinner.
9:00	Return to Alice Springs.

Leaving Melbourne
Flemington Road leads north into the Calder Highway, taking you to Melbourne International Airport at Tullamarine. Arrive well before your flight departure to turn in your rental car.

Alice Springs Orientation
With a rapidly growing population of about 25,000, "The Alice" is the biggest town for more than 800 miles in any direction. A desert oasis, it is situated in the midst of the MacDonnel Ranges, almost exactly in the geographic center of the continent. Australians call this area "The Centre" (or "The Red Centre" because of the unusual color of its soil).

Founded in 1872 as a station on the Overland Telegraph Line between Adelaide and Darwin, it got its name when station-master Charles Todd dubbed a permanent waterhole in the bed of the usually dry Todd River "Alice Springs" after his wife. When the railroad came through in 1929, the population was still only 200. A road from Adelaide was completed about 1940; only in April 1987 was the final link paved. The population didn't reach 1,000 until the 1950s or 5,000 until the 1970s. Modern tourism, however, has contributed to a boom throughout the Northern Territory, especially in The Alice.

The central business district is a compact 12 square blocks between the highway and the Todd River, bounded by Wills Terrace on the north and Stott Terrace on the south. The Todd Street Mall, recently made a pedestrians-only thoroughfare, stretches for two blocks from Gregory Terrace to Wills Terrace a block west of the river and is regarded as the center of town. (It is bisected by Parsons Street and is paralleled to the west by Hartley and Bath streets and to the east by Leichhardt Terrace overlooking the river.)

The word "river," by the way, is a misnomer. To be called a "local" in Alice Springs, one must have seen the Todd flow its length three times. Some 20-year residents are still waiting to become locals. The river is completely dry most of the year.

The Northern Territory Government Tourist Bureau, 51 Todd St. at Parsons St. (tel. 52-1299), has a wide selection of maps, brochures, and other information, including detailed walking and driving tours of the city area.

City Transportation

Alice Springs Airport is some 14 km (9 miles) south of the city center. Pay A$3.50 (A$5 return) for shuttle service up the Stuart Highway to downtown.

There's no public transportation in Alice Springs except for taxis, and they're rather expensive. If you want to get out and see the town—beyond what you can easily walk to—you have these options:

1.) Rent a car for the day. You can get an open "moke" for as little as A$17 a day and 18 cents a km, plus $5 for insurance. (That's a cost of A$31 if you do 50 km of driving.) A compact will run A$25 a day and 18 cents a km.

2.) Hire a car and driver, at a rate of A$35 for two hours. The Northern Territory Government Tourist Bureau has a list of operators.

3.) Join a bus tour. Three-hour tours operated by Ansett and AAT King's, among others, are priced at A$22, including all admissions.

4.) Rent a bicycle or moped. Thrifty Bike Hire on Todd Street has bikes for A$6 for an 8-hour day, mopeds for A$20 a day. The tourist bureau can tell you about other locations.

Sightseeing Highlights

Anzac Hill, named in honor of the combined World War I and II armed forces of Australia and New Zealand, offers a good view of Alice Springs and the surrounding terrain. Drive the circular road off Stuart Highway, or hike the steep Lions Walk from the end of Bath Street off Wills Terrace.

▲▲**The Old Telegraph Station** is 3 km north of Alice Springs off the Stuart Highway. The reserve has restored the original 1872 telegraph station and equipment and displays early photographs and historical documents. There are nature walks and a small wildlife park nearby, as well as a picnic ground and barbecue area beside the Alice Springs waterhole.

▲**The School of the Air** provides education by short-wave radio to children through the Central Australian outback, some as far as 1,000 km (621 miles) away. Visitors are invited to observe and listen between 1:30 and 3:30 p.m. on school days (Monday to Friday except holidays). The school is located beside Braitling School in Head Street, about 1½ miles north of downtown.

▲▲**The Royal Flying Doctor Service** was established in 1939 by the Rev. John Flynn, probably The Alice's best-known historical figure, to deliver medical attention to isolated homesteads by small plane. Today it relies more on radio communication to serve thousands of square miles from New South Wales and Queensland to Western Australia. Tours of the base, near the south end of Bath Street on Stuart Terrace, are offered every half-hour from 9:00 to 11:30 a.m. and 2:00 to 3:30 p.m. Monday to Friday, and from 9:00 to 11:00 a.m. Saturday. Admission is A$1.50. (Flynn's original aircraft is on display at the Aviation Museum on Memorial Drive, at the old Alice Springs airport.)

▲**Panorama Guth**, 65 Hartley St. north of Stott Terrace, is the private gallery of painter Henk Guth, who has created an unusual 360-degree mural of the terrain surrounding Alice Springs. Guth also has a collection of photographs, Aboriginal artifacts, and watercolor paintings of the Hermannsburg School. Open 9:00 a.m. to 5:00 p.m. Monday to Friday, 9:00 a.m. to noon and 2:00 to 5:00 p.m. Saturday, 2:00 to 5:00 p.m. Sunday. Admission is A$1.50.

▲**Pitchi Richi Sanctuary**, on Aranda Terrace south of Heavitree Gap near the Todd River causeway, combines William Ricketts' unique Aboriginal-theme sculpture with an outdoor folk museum and wild bird refuge. If you missed the Ricketts Sanctuary in the Dandenong Ranges east of Melbourne, don't miss this. Open daily 9:00 a.m. to sunset. Admission is A$1.50.

▲**Diorama Village**, 2 km west of downtown on Larapinta Drive at Bradshaw Drive, uses narrated dioramas to depict Aboriginal myths—like how the kangaroo got his tail and how the Milky Way was formed. Open 10:00 a.m. to 5:00 p.m. daily; admission A$2.

▲Aboriginal art galleries exhibit and sell the arts and crafts of the native tribes of Central Australia—the Arunta, the Curindji, and the Pitjantjatjara. Browse at the government-operated **Centre for Aboriginal Artists and Craftsmen**, 86 Todd St., or any of a dozen other shops and galleries.

Frontier Camel Farm, 4 km south of town on Emily Gap Road (the Ross Highway), is open for riding these "ships of the desert" from 8:00 a.m. to 5:00 p.m. daily. It also has a Magic Spark Museum of early radio communications. Admission is A$2.50.

The **Mecca Date Garden** on Emily Gap Road is Australia's only commercial date garden, with 20 varieties of productive date palms. Open daily 9:30 a.m. to 4:30 p.m. Admission, including a conducted tour, is A$1.50.

▲**The Henley-on-Todd Regatta** is perhaps the most exciting boating race never to take place on water. Every year on the last weekend of August, 40-foot yachts line up in the dry riverbed, gripped tightly on the gunwale by their crews, who run with them as fast as they can. It's a good excuse for a party.

Where to Stay

The top of the line in Alice Springs is represented by the modern **Sheraton Alice Springs**, Barrett Drive (tel. 52-8000), followed closely by its next-door neighbor, **Lasseter's Casino** (tel. 52-5066). Both are on the south side of town. The **Elkira Motel**, 134 Bath St. (tel. 52-1222); the **Desert Rose Inn**, 15 Railway Terrace (tel. 52-1411); and the **Oasis Motel**, 10 Gap Road at Traeger Avenue (tel. 52-1444), are centrally located and moderately priced.

For economy lodging, try the **Arura Safari Lodge**, 18 Warburton St. at Lindsay Avenue (tel. 52-3843). The YWCA's **Stuart Lodge**, Stuart Terrace near Todd Street (tel. 52-1894), takes both men and women.

Budget travelers can get a cheap bed at the **Sandrifter Safari Lodge**, 6 Kharlic St. (tel. 52-8686), or the **Alice Springs Youth Hostel** at the corner of Todd Street and Stott Terrace (tel. 52-5016).

Where to Eat

Aside from hotel coffee shops and restaurants, there is a good variety of dining establishments in Alice Springs. Steak and spicy food lovers appreciate **Overlanders Steakhouse**, 72 Hartley St., with meals in the A$8 to A$10 range. Ask for buffalo steak in witchety grub sauce. **The Todd Tavern**, at the corner of the Todd Street Mall and Wills Terrace, has several restaurants, including **The Other Place**, serving counter meals priced from A$4.50 and the more formal **Maxim's** for continental cuisine.

Chopsticks,in the Ermond Arcade on Hartley Street, is the local Chinese favorite with Cantonese and Szechuan cuisine. Good, cheap breakfasts and lunches cost no more than A$5 at the **Eranova Cafeteria**, 72 Todd St.

Fifteen km (9½ miles) south of Alice Springs is **Chateau Hornsby**, Central Australia's first and only winery. The wine isn't great, but it's certainly palatable—and dry! There's an informal outdoor barbecue area, fine for lunches, and a pleasant indoor restaurant, where local bush balladeer Ted Egan performs most nights. Find it at the end of Petrick Road, off Colonel Rose Drive.

On Sundays, Tuesdays, and Fridays, for A$50, you can "Take a Camel to Dinner" by joining **Frontier Tours**' sundown safari down the Todd River bed to Chateau Hornsby. The price includes an hour on a camel's back and a five-course barramundi (fish) or buffalo roast dinner. The beasts leave Alice Springs at 4:00 p.m. (returning at 9:00 p.m.) October to April and depart at 3:00 p.m. May to September. Book at your hotel or call 53-0444.

Nightlife

Alice Springs isn't Sydney or Melbourne. But it does have a casino. **Lasseter's Casino** on Barrett Drive, on the southeast side of town, is named after Harold Lasseter, a local legend who perished in the desert searching for a fabled reef of gold in 1931. Harry should have lived so long; the gold is here, on the gaming tables. The casino also has a disco open Thursday 11:00 p.m. to 4:00 a.m., Friday and Saturday 11:00 p.m. to 5:00 a.m.

There's live music Thursday to Sunday at the **Todd Tavern**, Wills Terrace and Todd Street Mall, and the **Stuart Arms Hotel**, Parsons Street and Todd Street Mall. **Bojangles Nightclub**, Todd Street near Stott Terrace, is open nightly except Sunday for meals and disco dancing 'til the wee hours.

If there's more upscale entertainment in town, you'll find it at the **Araluen Arts Centre**, west of downtown on Larapinta Drive. The Alice's center for the performing and visual arts attracts name entertainers from Australia and overseas.

ALICE SPRINGS TO AYERS ROCK

Marvel at the weird geology of the Red Centre as you fly from
Alice Springs to Yulara resort village at Ayers Rock, arriving in
the early afternoon. After getting settled in your lodging and
exploring the community, join the sunset barbecue tour to the
Olgas.

Suggested Schedule

9:00	You'll have time to do some shopping or sight-seeing in Alice Springs before taking a shuttle bus to the airport.
11:00	Ansett N.T. Flight BT278 for Ayers Rock.
11:45	Arrive at Ayers Rock's Connellan Airport.
12:15	Get settled in your accommodations, take a dip in the pool, eat lunch, then drop by the Yulara Visitors Centre and tour the resort complex.
4:30	Depart on "outback" barbecue tour to the Olgas.
9:30	Return to hotel.

Ayers Rock Orientation

The great red monolith of Ayers Rock is the symbol of the Australian outback, at once an irresistible spiritual force to the
Aboriginal people and a testimony to the stark, primeval beauty
of the desert landscape.

There is no larger rock on earth. Yet Ayers Rock may not be
as well known for its massive size (1,260 feet high, 5 ½ miles
around its base) as for its moods. From dawn to dusk, the Rock
undergoes a continuous series of subtle color changes, from
sunrise pink to midday brown, sunset red to postsunset purple.
During the rare desert downpours, it can even appear silvery
with rain cascading down its time-sculpted slopes.

The ancient Loritja and Pitjantjatjara tribes called the Rock
"Uluru." Thousands of years ago, they decorated the cave
walls around its base with paintings and petroglyphs. Not until
1872 did Europeans know of the Rock; Ernest Giles sighted it
during his explorations of the Centre, and the following year,
William Gosse led a three-month camel caravan to climb the
monolith. Today, the ascent is a relatively simple, if strenuous,
morning excursion.

About 510 square miles surrounding Ayers Rock and the nearby Olgas range—piled high like a giant's marbles above the sandy earth—were established in 1958 as Ayers Rock-Mount Olga National Park. Title for the parklands was transferred to the Aboriginal people in 1985, and Uluru National Park came into being. Commercial enterprise—motels, a campground, and an airstrip—was moved out of the shadow of the Rock.

Yulara, 19 km (12 miles) from Ayers Rock, was built to provide comfort in the desert sun for the rapidly growing influx of tourists. Only 2,300 people visited Ayers Rock when the national park first opened in 1958; but by 1987, with a sealed, 468 km (291 miles) all-weather road linking the Rock to Alice Springs, Uluru was attracting 220,000 visitors from all over the world—despite being one of the costliest destinations in Australia.

The resort village, completed in 1984, can accommodate up to 5,000 people a day in two luxury hotels, a midpriced lodge, and a spacious campground. And it is a complete village—in fact, with its resident population of around 500, it is the third largest community in the sparsely settled Northern Territory (after Darwin and Alice Springs). There's a small shopping square, a school, a medical center, a community hall and sports center, a police station, and other facilities to keep the people from feeling too isolated.

Still, they must cope with the summer heat and year-round temperature extremes. From December to February, daytime temperatures average about 97 degrees Fahrenheit, dropping to around 70 at night; midwinter temperatures range from average daytime highs of 58 to nighttime lows of 41, though freezing temperatures are not uncommon. Total rainfall is only 10 inches a year, with February the wettest month (1 ½ inches) and September the driest (¼ inch).

Yulara Transportation

There isn't any cheap way to get around here, short of walking. The shuttle bus for the short hop from the airport to Yulara costs A$5 one way; the price of the three-times-a-day shuttle from the resort to Ayers Rock is A$12 return, or about 50 cents a mile. And so it goes. **Deluxe Coachline** has the concession. Some visitors find the three-day "Rock Pass," allowing unlimited trips on the shuttle buses to the Rock and the Olgas, a worthwhile purchase at A$39.

Cars are available for rent, but they're hardly a bargain. If the weather cooperates—and it usually does—consider hiring a moped from the Mobil Service Station in Yulara village. Half-day (four-hour) rental is A$20, full-day A$30.

Where to Stay
The **Sheraton Ayers Rock Hotel** (tel. 56-2200) is the luxury
leader, with 230 rooms rambling around a lovely swimming
pool and courtyard. Twin rooms are A$135 a night. Many visi-
tors prefer the A$120 rooms across the village at the **Four Sea-
sons Ayers Rock Motel** (tel. 56-2100). More moderately
priced are the Yulara Mansionettes (tel. 56-2131), with A$86
twins. The **Ayers Rock Lodge** (tel. 56-2170) offers bare-bones
family units or cabins for four at A$48, hostel-style dorm
accommodations at A$12 a bunk.

Where to Eat
The **Sheraton** has two fine restaurants, the **Four Seasons**
another. At either hotel, you can get a filling buffet dinner for
around A$25. There are three less expensive options, perhaps
the best being the counter meals and buffet at the **Ernest Giles
Tavern**, open daily in the Shopping Square. The adjacent **Old
Oak Tree Coffee Shop** has light meals and takeaways, while
the **Ayers Rock Lodge Food Bar** is popular for its casual
home cooking.

Sightseeing Highlight
▲▲**The Olgas**, to many visitors, are even more spectacular
than Ayers Rock itself. An accumulation of 36 oddly shaped
domes that rise from the Central Australian desert some 32 km
(20 miles) west of the Rock, they were known to the Aboriginals as Katatjuta and feared as hungry giants. Indeed, the Olgas
can be sirens who lure explorers into their seductive wonder-
land only to cook them alive in a midday oven. In 1987, foreign
visitors died in the Olgas on two separate occasions.

By late afternoon, the heat is off again. One way to appreciate
these geological curiosities is with the Ayers Rock Touring
Company's "Evening in the Outback" tour. You'll be picked
up in Yulara about 4:30 p.m., head out to the west side of the
Olgas to watch the colorful sunset, then drive to an isolated
spot for a "steak-and-snags" barbecue under the Southern
Cross. If you shine a flashlight toward the darkness around
your campfire, you may see the shining eyes of wild dingoes
waiting to feast on your leftovers. The tour's major drawback is
its price—A$39, not acceptable on the Rock Pass. (Hours are a
half-hour later from mid-October through March.)

Nightlife
A bush band performs Aussie sing-along and dance music most
nights in the Sheraton's **Mulgara Bar**. It's good fun, the best
reason to visit the Sheraton if you're not staying there. The
Ernest Giles Tavern has a pub disco several nights of the week.

AYERS ROCK

Learn about the Aboriginal culture today. Spend the morning with a native guide who will show you how his people found food, water, shelter, and medicine in this arid landscape. Visit the craft exhibit at the Uluru National Park ranger station and search for ancient petroglyphs in caves around the base of Ayers Rock. Back at Yulara, sip champagne as you watch the sun set over the red rock.

Suggested Schedule	
7:00	Leave Yulara via shuttle bus for Ayers Rock.
7:30	While others are beginning their ascent, stroll to Maggie Springs, then to the ranger station.
8:30	"Liru" walk with Aboriginal guide.
10:45	Return to the ranger station to see the outdoor exhibit of Aboriginal crafts and video.
12:15	Back to Yulara aboard shuttle bus.
1:00	Lunch, swim, relax.
Open	Go to the Sheraton lookout tower 45 minutes before sunset to sip champagne and watch the Rock's colors change. Then dinner.
9:00	Early bedtime for tomorrow's "ordeal."

Sightseeing Highlights
▲▲**Maggie Springs**, known to the Pitjantjatjara as Mutitjulu, is a deep, tranquil pool nestled against the southeast wall of Ayers Rock. After a rainstorm, you can often see tiny desert frogs and fairy shrimp in the water. The hideaway is especially striking in the late morning, when the blue of the outback sky contrasts sharply with the red of the rock and the green of the mulga and desert oak vegetation. Nearby are several small caves, their walls and roofs adorned with Aboriginal cave paintings thousands of years old. Maggie Springs are a level 2½-km walk from the shuttle bus stop.

▲▲**The Liru Walk** only happens twice a week, but it's worth catching when it does. Beginning at 8:30 a.m. Tuesdays and Thursdays, an Aboriginal woman (females are the traditional food-gatherers in Central Australia) leads a group from the Uluru National Park Ranger Station on a two-hour bush walk to demonstrate how her people survived in this arid climate using only natural food sources. You'll learn, for instance, that the

Central Australia

burrowing witchety grub is superb food, 50% protein and 50% fat; that the fruit of the plumbush tree has the highest known concentration of vitamin C; that the prolific mulga tree has seeds that can be ground to make flour; and that the flowers of the hakea tree, mixed with water, make a drink similar to cola. And remember that scene in *Crocodile Dundee* where Mick skewers a large lizard for dinner? Your guide will show you where to find a tasty sand goanna just like it.

In fact, there is a bewildering variety of wildlife here in the desert. Naturalists have counted 290 species of plant life, 151 birds, 52 reptiles, and 22 native mammals. The most prolific of all creatures is the blowfly, sort of a larger, more persistent version of the American housefly. Without direct sunlight, and with a bit of a breeze, they're not bad. In most circumstances, they're extremely unpleasant. You'll soon learn why "The Great Australian Salute" is a hand waving past your face to keep these flies out of your eyes, nose, ears, and mouth.

Flies notwithstanding, the Liru Walk is a fascinating look at a life-style very different from our own. Tour numbers are limited, so book ahead by phoning 56-2988. The tour concludes at the base of the Rock climb, leaving a 20-minute return walk to the ranger station.

▲**Uluru National Park Ranger Station**, where everyone who enters the park is supposed to stop and pay a A$1.50 use fee, has a number of exhibits of special interest to the park visitor. In particular, take some time to talk with the Aboriginal people displaying local, handmade arts and crafts in a special outdoor area.

AYERS ROCK TO WALLARA RANCH

If the world's largest monolith is awesome at sunset, it's even more stunning at dawn. Awaken early to watch the spectacle and to beat the heat and flies as you scale the huge red rock. Then you too can wear a T-shirt declaring, "I Climbed Ayers Rock." After lunch, board a bus for the 125-mile drive to Wallara Ranch, where you'll spend the night at an outback station.

Suggested Schedule

6:45	Leave Yulara via shuttle bus for Ayers Rock.
7:30	Begin climb up Ayers Rock. Allow 90 minutes for the return trip.
9:00	Tour base of Rock by bus or take the ranger-guided hike to Kantju Gorge.
11:45	Return to Yulara via shuttle bus. Lunch.
1:30	Farewell to Ayers Rock.
3:30	Rest stop at Angas Downs turnoff.
5:30	Arrive Wallara Ranch for overnight stay.

Sightseeing Highlights

▲▲▲ Climbing Ayers Rock is a must, as long as you're in reasonably good physical condition. The ever-cautious national park administration warns that the average time of climbing the 1.6 km (1 mile) to the cairn and returning to the foot of the Rock is two hours. As a slightly out-of-shape, over-the-hill hiker, I can accomplish it in a little over an hour, including 15 minutes or so relaxing and taking photos at the top. But don't push yourself too hard; if you feel exhausted or nauseous, quit. Take a break, then head back down.

The first 500 meters of the climb are the steepest. A staunch chain has been sunk into the Rock to provide a handhold for any and all who need it while ascending the 45- to 60-degree angle. Once that portion has been surmounted, it's merely an uphill walk, with just a couple of precipitous drops and rises across eroded ridges.

At the top, you'll be rewarded with an unfettered view of hundreds of miles of red dirt. Be sure to sign the climbers' register, noting the vast array of nationalities who have put their home address there next to your own. After a short rest, you can head back down. Your calves got a workout on the way up;

now your thighs will feel it. Some climbers find it easier to back down the chain on the steepest stretch.

The best shoes for climbing are rubber soled. Any kind of athletic shoes work as well as proper climbing boots. Don't go in street shoes, thongs, or bare feet. Bring something with you to drink, and if you're starting much later than 8:00 a.m., put on suntan lotion and a sun hat. The wind can be stiff, so be sure to tie down anything you carry—or it may wind up at the bottom of the Rock long before you do.

▲**Circling the Rock** aboard the shuttle bus can be done if you're back at the base by 9:00 a.m. The driver-guide points out Taputji (Little Ayers Rock), Maggie Springs, and other sites around the Rock's circumference en route back to Yulara. It's interesting to note how different Ayers Rock appears from different viewpoints. The tour costs A$15, including the A$12 shuttle fee from Yulara.

▲**Ranger-guided walks**, which also leave at 9:00 a.m. from the car park at the base of the Rock climb, are free. For over an hour, hikers accompany a park ranger into Kantju Gorge, a cleft in the Rock with an adjacent waterhole. The ranger explains Ayers Rock's place in Aboriginal legend and tells about the geology and environment of this Central Australian region.

▲▲**Ayers Rock-Kings Canyon tours** are conducted by several tour companies based in Alice Springs. Any Northern Territory Government Tourist Bureau can provide a complete listing. I like the low-budget tour offered by A-1/Spinifex Tours (write Fan Arcade, Todd Street Mall, Alice Springs, NT 5750, tel., 089/52-5424 or 52-2203). But its tours are Saturday-to-Monday and Tuesday-to-Thursday expeditions, not helpful to those of us leaving Yulara on a Friday. My second choise is Ansett Trailways (Todd and Parsons streets, Alice Springs, NT 5750, tel. 089/52-2422), which has daily departures on the three-day Alice-Ayers Rock-Kings Canyon-Alice circuit. The trick is to join a tour in progress on departure from Yulara. Advance arrangements are essential.

You'll leave Yulara on the Lasseter Highway, a 247-km (153-mile) thoroughfare connecting Ayers Rock with the Stuart Highway, the main north-south route from Adelaide to Darwin. About 138 km (86 miles) from Yulara, following a rest stop at the Curtin Springs homestead and a view of isolated Mount Connor, you'll turn north past Angas Downs to the Wallara Ranch, 70 km (43 miles) farther.

Wallara Ranch offers bunkhouse and private, four-to-a-room cabin accommodations for economy prices. There's also a dining room with filling country-style meals.

WALLARA RANCH TO ALICE SPRINGS

Scramble through the sheer walls of colorful Kings Canyon, then return to Alice Springs in the evening. If you're not totally exhausted, enjoy a nightcap at the casino.

Suggested Schedule

6:00	Rise and shine; eat breakfast.
7:00	Leave for Kings Canyon.
9:00	Explore the spectacular chasm. Wander through the lush Garden of Eden and climb to the canyon rim for marvelous panoramic views.
11:30	Leave Kings Canyon.
1:30	Lunch at Wallara Ranch.
3:00	Leave for Alice Springs.
5:00	See the Henbury Craters.
6:30	Arrive at Alice Springs for the night.

Sightseeing Highlights
▲▲▲ **Kings Canyon**—Australia's spectacular "Grand Canyon" is a deep cleft in the George Gill Ranges, about 250 km—155 air miles—southwest of Alice Springs. (From the Wallara Ranch, it's a 99-km, or 61-mile, drive each way.)

Sheer sandstone walls rising 700 to 900 feet above the canyon floor vary in hue from pink to crimson, ivory to deep purple. In the Garden of Eden, lush palms grow around dozens of waterholes, reflecting the multicolored walls like so many kaleidoscopes. In the Lost City, rocky outcrops look like primitive rock dwellings of a forgotten tribe. The Sphinx is another formation unique in this terrain. You may find rock wallabies and goanna lizards at the waterholes, and you'll certainly see rose-tinted galahs and a variety of other birds. It's a steep climb to the canyon rim—more difficult than the struggle up Ayers Rock—but the panoramic views from the summit make the climb worthwhile. As at the Rock, you should wear rubber-soled shoes for climbing, apply suntan lotion, wear a sun hat, and carry something to drink.

Kings Canyon Road runs the 198 km (123 miles) from the canyon to the Stuart Highway, via the midway stop at Wallara Ranch. This is a graded-dirt road, typical of the outback. Tour bus drivers who ply this route regularly have taken all appropriate precautions for outback travel, but if you're driving yourself, you should follow the old Boy Scout axiom and "Be Prepared."

Watch out for road flooding, particularly where it crosses the Palmer River. This arid land doesn't absorb rainfall quickly, so even a half-inch of precipitation can have a major effect on road conditions. Beware of collisions with kangaroos, wild camels, and brumbies (wild horses). Carry water—at least a gallon per person per day of your trip—plus reserve gas, a tool kit, two spare tires, and extra engine parts. It helps if you have a mechanical inclination.

▲**Henbury Craters** are an odd cluster of about a dozen meteor craters off Kings Canyon Road near its junction with the Stuart Highway, 132 km (82 miles) south of Alice Springs. Between 2,000 and 3,000 years ago, a shower of meteorites rained down on this 40-acre conservation park, creating craters from 20 to 600 feet across and as much as 50 feet deep. A walking trail from the car park signposts many of the features.

▲**The Virginia Camel Farm**, 90 km (56 miles) south of The Alice, is Noel Fullerton's contribution to Central Australian culture. Fullerton originated Alice Springs' Lions Club "Camel Cup" in the 1970s, won it himself four times, and now has placed his teenage children in the championship category of camel-riding. (The Cup races are held annually in May.) The farm domesticates some of the Centre's estimated 15,000 wild camels and breeds others for export to—of all places—the Arab world, from which Australia's herd originated! Visitors can pay a few dollars for a short camel ride or book a one- or two-week safari east into the Rainbow Valley.

ALICE SPRINGS TO CAIRNS

Today, fly from Alice Springs to Cairns. On arrival in Cairns, the humidity will tell you immediately that you're in the tropics. Have a cold beer at an Esplanade pub, watch the fishing and pleasure boats return from the Great Barrier Reef, see the Reef World aquarium. For dinner, order barramundi, a delectable river-run cod.

Suggested Schedule	
8:30	Leisurely breakfast at hotel, then take a shuttle bus to the airport.
10:55	Ansett Flight 285 to Cairns.
1:20	Arrive at Cairns International Airport. Take a shuttle bus 8 km to town and check into hotel.
3:00	Stroll down the Esplanade and around town. See the Reef World aquarium, the marlin jetty, and perhaps the museum or House of 10,000 Shells.
6:30	Dinner at one of Cairns' fine seafood eateries.

Cairns Orientation
Cairns (don't pronounce the "r") is the undeclared capital of lazy, tropical North Queensland. A rapidly growing town of about 70,000 people on the shores of Trinity Bay, it is wedged against a backdrop of rain forest-clad mountains, facing the so-called eighth wonder of the world, the Great Barrier Reef.

Founded in the mid-1870s as a customs collection point and a port for gold and tin mines in the interior of Queensland, it later grew as a center for sugarcane growing and processing. Sugar and tin remain economically important today, along with fishing, timber, and tropical fruit.

But tourism is taking over as the No. 1 revenue producer. From 1979 to 1984, the number of tourists coming to this lush location more than doubled, and there are indications that the number could redouble by 1990. Eighteen new hotels with over 3,600 rooms were built in the greater Cairns area between 1985 and 1988. The Cairns airport now has direct flight connections with nearby Papua New Guinea and with the U.S. West Coast, making it more accessible to tourists than ever before.

Why do the tourists come? The primary reason is the reef. No population center along the Australian coast is closer to the coral phenomenon than Cairns, with Green Island a mere 40-minute launch trip away. Second, they come for the fishing. Cairns is famed for its sportfishing fleet; international celebrities use Cairns as a base for marlin fishing. Third, they come for the jungle. Some of the last great tracts of rain forest on earth are west of Cairns on the Atherton Tableland and north around Cape Tribulation.

Cairns itself is an easy town to find your way around. It's stereotypically tropical, its ornate, wide-verandahed homes often raised well above the ground for air circulation. The streets are wide and palm fringed, the harbor a bustling center of trade amid squawking seabirds. Spence Street runs due west from the marlin jetty; it's paralleled to the north by Shields, Aplin, Florence, Minnie, and Upward streets. The Esplanade, which runs along the shore from Upward to Spence, and McLeod Street, which fronts the railroad tracks, mark the eastern and western boundaries of the downtown district. Abbott, Lake, Grafton and Sheridan streets run between, from east to west. City Place, a mall marking the center of the city, is at the intersection of Shields and Lake. Sheridan Street is the main thoroughfare north toward the airport and the Cook Highway.

City Transportation

A regular shuttle-bus service operates between Cairns International Airport and town, a distance of 8 km (5 miles), for A$3. (Leaving town, call 53-4722 for pickup times.) Taxi fare between Cairns and the airport is about A$7.

If you arrived in Cairns by train from Brisbane or other points south, you'll disembark at Cairns Station on McLeod Street, at the end of Shields Street. All downtown points are within easy walking distance. (The economy single adult rail fare from Brisbane to Cairns, one way, is A$84.80. Trains arrive Tuesday through Friday plus Sunday at 7:45 p.m.; the Queenslander express comes in Monday only at 5:55 p.m.)

A variety of bus services are available within and around Cairns at reasonable fares. (Schedules are posted in the foyer of the O.T. Corporation and on the window of Rockman's, both on Shield Street between City Place and Abbott Street.) There are interstate bus terminals for Greyhound at 78 Grafton St. and Ansett Pioneer at 58 Shields St.

Car rentals are also readily available in town and at the airport. For cheap moke or moped rentals, check with Mini Car Rental, 143 Sheridan St. You can rent bicycles in several locations, including Cycle Works, Aplin and Lake streets, and the Bicycle Barn, 61 Sheridan St.

Where to Stay

With all those new hotels, and some three dozen others, there are a wide variety of accommodations available in Cairns. Generally speaking, you'll find the budget and moderate lodging in the town itself. Luxury hotels are often up the coast, among them **Ramada Reef Resort** at Palm Cove (tel. 070/55-3999), about 25 km (16 miles) north of Cairns. The A$150 million **Sheraton Mirage Resort**, 76 km (47 miles) from Cairns at Port Douglas, has an 18-hole championship golf course and Hovercraft connection to Cairns International Airport.

The No. 1 hotel in Cairns is the **Pacific International Hotel**, 43 The Esplanade (tel. 070/51-7888), with three restaurants, three bars, and a health club. Its preeminence will soon be challenged by a new Hilton and a new Park Royal.

In the moderate price class, it would be hard to do better than the **Cairns Colonial Club**, 18-26 Cannon St. (tel. 53-5111), which surmounts the minor drawback of being a couple miles north of the city center with regular free shuttle service. A choice of rooms at several price levels starting at A$49 are nestled around an open-air restaurant-bar and saltwater pool, complete with sandy beach and waterfall.

Economy travelers will do well at the **Silver Palms Private Hotel**, 153 The Esplanade (tel. 51-2059), and the **Linga Longa**, 223 The Esplanade (tel. 51-3013), both equipped with kitchens. And those touring on a shoestring will quickly learn why Cairns is becoming one of the budget travel capitals of the world. The biggest of five hostels is **Caravella's**, 77-81 The Esplanade (tel. 51-2159). There are others on The Esplanade at No. 67 and No. 149. A bit quieter is the **Cairns Backpackers Inn**, 255 Lake St. (tel. 51-9166).

Sightseeing Highlights

Once you're settled, it's time to see the sights of town. Cairns is better known as a base for excursions to the reef and inland, but these will fill an afternoon.

▲▲**The Marlin Jetty** is a "must" stop during the sportfishing season, which runs from August into December. When private boats and charter operators return here toward evening with their days' catches, the heart of even the veteran fisherman has to thump a little. Black marlin, hoisted onto the scales, may go well over the 1,000-pound mark.

▲**Reef World** is an aquarium on Marlin Parade with a variety of saltwater species—crocodiles, turtles, sharks, giant clams, and a great many fish, including barramundi, huge groupers, and the poisonous stonefish. There's even a stingray who is fed by hand every day at 2:00 p.m. Open daily from 10:00 a.m. to 5:30 p.m.; admission is A\$3.

▲**Windows on the Reef**, located off Wharf Street on the Great Barrier Reef cruise docks, simulates a night dive on the reef from within a small rotating theater. The 45-minute show is a good introduction to the massive coral creation not far off-shore. Open daily 10:00 a.m. to 5:30 p.m. Admission is A\$4.

▲**The Cairns Museum**, located in an early twentieth-century School of Arts building at the corner of Lake and Shields streets, has displays of natural history, North Queensland Aboriginal artifacts, gold-mining (and early Chinese habitation), and railway construction. Open 10:00 a.m. to 3:00 p.m. Monday to Friday. Admission is A\$1.

The House of 10,000 Shells, 32-34 Abbott St., is a glorified souvenir shop with an interesting collection of shells from every corner of the globe. Open daily; admission is free.

Laroc Coral Jewellery Factory, about 3 km from the Cairns town center at 82 Aumuller St., presents a workshop-viewing area and a 10-minute video on the making of coral jewelry. Open daily; admission is free.

Cairns Botanical Gardens, Collins Avenue in Edge Hill, two miles from the town center, comprise a luxuriant century-old tropical jungle and parkland with more than 10,000 species of trees, shrubs, and flowers. There's a great view across Cairns to Trinity Bay from the top of Mount Whitfield. Open daily sunrise to sunset. Admission is free.

Where to Eat

For a relatively small city, Cairns offers an awesome variety of international cuisine in its many restaurants.

Some of the licensed seafood restaurants have the most style. Try **Scuppers**, Grafton and Aplin streets; **Fathoms**, Grove and Diggers streets (near Grafton), especially for the garlic chili crab; or **Tawny's** on the Marlin Jetty. **Lin Nam**, 14 Aplin St., has good Chinese seafood. An excellent BYO seafood eatery is **Avocado**, 228 Sheridan St.

Among other BYO restaurants, these are a few of the best, by cuisine: **Der Feinschmecker** (German), 95 Grafton St.; **Thuggee Bill's** (Indian), 42 Aplin St.; **Toko Baru** (Indonesian), 42 Spence St.; **Omar Khayyam** (Lebanese), 82 Sheridan St.; **Rahmah's** (Malaysian), 47 Shields St.; **Little Gringo** (Mexican), 95 Grafton St.; **Casa Gomez** (Spanish), 48 Aplin St.; **Sweethearts** (vegetarian); and **Rusty's Bazaar** on Grafton Street.

Along the Esplanade and around the City Place mall, several restaurants have outdoor tables set up to catch the eyes and noses of passersby. One of the most popular for lunch is **Swagman's Rest**, City Place.

Last, but far from least, is the **Backpackers' Restaurant** on Shields Street just east of City Place. With a name like that, its clientele is—you guessed it—mainly backpackers. And it's always packed. Counter meals are cheap and good, beer is cheap and good, and both are served into the wee hours.

Nightlife

The scene changes often in a resort town like Cairns, but at this writing, the favored upscale nightclubs were the **Playpen International**, 2 Lake St.; **Scandals**, in the Tradewinds Sunlodge at Lake and Florence streets; and the **House on the Hill**, Kingsford Street in out-of-the-way Mooroobool. All are open until 3:00 in the morning, although nights of closing vary.

Close to the city center, and more in the vein of a quieter drink and conversation to a piano bar or light jazz, are **The Nest**, 82 McLeod St.; **Duke's**, upstairs at 86 Lake St.; and **Kipling's Wine Bar**, 79 Abbott St.

Young rockers find loud music and cheap drinks at the **Hideaway Tavern**, Lake Street between Spence and Shield. **Hides Hotel**, at the southwest corner of City Place, is always good for a rage. You'll often find the fishermen in the **Marlin Bar** at the Great Northern Hotel, 69 Abbott St.

You might also get a kick out of **Milliway's**, an upstairs BYO built around the theme of Douglas Adams' spacey novel, *A Hitchhikers' Guide to the Galaxy*. This BYO café upstairs at 144 Grafton St. offers a place where any traveling musician can drop by to jam for all he (or she) is worth.

Helpful Hints

The two best sources of travel and touring information once you've arrived in Cairns are the Far North Queensland Promotion Bureau, corner of Sheridan and Aplin streets (tel. 51-3588), and the Queensland Government Travel Centre, 12 Shields St. (tel. 51-4066). Both are open weekdays 9:00 a.m. to 5:00 p.m.

The General Post Office is on the corner of Florence and Sheridan streets. Banks stay open from 9:30 a.m. to 4:00 p.m. Monday to Thursday, to 5:00 p.m. Friday. Retail shops in the downtown area open 8:30 a.m. to 5:15 p.m. Monday to Thursday, to 9:00 p.m. Friday, to noon Saturday.

In case of emergencies, dial 000.

GREEN ISLAND

Ship out for Green Island, a tiny coral cay 40 minutes' cruise offshore where you can swim, study sea life from a glass-bottom boat, view the world's largest crocodile in captivity, and dine, drink, and sleep at the small resort.

Suggested Schedule

7:00	Breakfast at hotel. Stow whatever bags you won't need on the island to await your return tomorrow night.
8:30	Leave for Green Island aboard Hayles' Cruises 220-passenger catamaran.
11:00	Walk around the island. It takes 20 minutes.
12:00	Lay on the beach some more.
1:00	Lunch, if you're ready.
2:30	Siesta.
3:30	Snorkeling again, or visit the croc.
6:00	Happy hour.
7:00	Dinner.

Alternative Schedule for Budget Travelers

9:00	Leave for Fitzroy Island aboard the MV *Fitzroy* catamaran.
9:45	Arrive at Fitzroy Island. Snorkel over the coral or go bushwalking in the rain forest.
1:00	Lunch. Rest of day on the beach at Fitzroy.

Sightseeing Highlights

▲▲▲ **Green Island** is a misnomer. It's green, all right, cloaked in lush palms, figs, and other rain forest vegetation, but at a mere 32 acres in size, and nowhere more than 10 feet in elevation, it's hardly classifiable as an island! In fact, you can walk around this isolated coral cay, 17 miles offshore from Cairns, in about 20 minutes.

But Green Island's miniature size is part of its charm. Most of the islet is reserved as a marine national park for its fine plant and bird life. It's completely fringed by a beach of fine white sand, and the offshore snorkeling is excellent.

Hayles' Cruises (tel. 51-5644) operates a transit service from the Green Island Jetty off Wharf Street opposite Abbott Street. Luxury catamarans—double-deckers complete with bars— leave at 8:30 and 10:30 a.m. daily on the 40-minute journey.

The adult fare is A$23 return. Ordinary launches leave at 9:00 a.m. daily, making the trip in 90 minutes for A$12 return.

Once on the island, what's there to do? Well, to begin with, there's that fabulous beach. Swim, snorkel, skindive, even try windsurfing. (Equipment is available for rent at reasonable rates on the beach.) You can try casting a line for reef fish or just communing with nature in the forest.

At the end of the boat jetty, anchored on the seabed, is the **Green Island Underwater Observatory**, where you can descend to the ocean floor to gaze through large viewing windows at luminescent tropical fish flitting through colorful banks of coral, itself inhabited by starfish, anemones, giant clams, and other undersea creatures. Admission is A$3.20.

On shore, **Marineland Melanesia** is an indoor-outdoor aquarium combined with a New Guinean artifact collection. It's worth visiting mainly to see its crocodiles. Well over a dozen of the ill-tempered reptiles are in residence here, including one Guinness-class monster nearly 20 feet long. He usually hides under his lily pads, but one glimpse of his huge jaws thrashing after a chunk of raw meat at feeding time will remind you why you should never go swimming alone in a saltwater estuary. Admission is A$3.50. Next door to this Marineland is the **Castaway Theatre**, which offers an underwater camera's perspective of the wonders of the Great Barrier Reef.

The comfortable **Green Island Reef Resort** has private lodging for A$54 to A$69 a night (A$10 more in the midsummer holiday season). The price includes dinner (usually a choice of meat or a reef fish) and a buffet breakfast. Lunch at the outdoor grill and drinks in the lounge are extra.

▲▲**Fitzroy Island** is a much larger island than Green—about 750 acres—but a much smaller resort. That makes it ideal for travelers seeking a bit of isolation.

Located 3½ miles off the coast 16 miles east of Cairns, this mountainous island is shrouded in tropical rain forest and fringed by rugged coral beaches. It's not great for sunbathing, but there's an excellent reef 150 feet offshore for snorkeling and diving. You can rent equipment for those sports as well as canoeing and paddle skiing. Or you can go off on your own long bushwalks through the dense vegetation.

The MV *Fitzroy* catamaran (A$11 return) leaves Cairns daily at 9:00 a.m., reaching Fitzroy at 9:45 a.m. It departs Fitzroy at 1:30 p.m. for passage back to Cairns via Green Island.

The **Fitzroy Island Resort** on Welcome Bay caters to budget travelers with hostel-style rooms (A$25 for two) with communal kitchens. It also has guest villas for A$79 full board (A$90 single). The licensed dining room specializes in seafood.

GREAT BARRIER REEF

You'll leave Green Island this morning to spend the day snorkeling or diving on the outer Barrier Reef. It is an incredible experience to see more than 200 species of tropical reef fish swimming through an undersea "garden" of multicolored coral. Return to Cairns at night.

Suggested Schedule

11:15	Leave Green Island aboard Hayles' Reef Cat for Michaelmas Cay and Hastings Reef.
12:15	Arrive at Hastings Reef.
3:15	Leave Hastings Reef.
5:15	Return to Cairns after 15-minute pickup and drop-off stop at Green Island.
5:30	Get reestablished at hotel.
6:30	Dinner, perhaps followed by tropical nightlife.

Alternative Schedule (for Fitzroy Island overnighters)

1:30	Depart Fitzroy Island.
2:00	Arrive Green Island.
4:30	Leave Green Island.
5:15	Return to Cairns. Remainder of day as above.

Sightseeing Highlights

▲▲▲ **The Great Barrier Reef** is truly one of the wonders of the world. Stretching for more than 2,000 km (1,250 miles) down the coast of Queensland from New Guinea to the Tropic of Capricorn, it is the largest structure (80,000 square miles of individual reefs, shoals, and islets) ever created by living creatures.

Tiny marine animals called polyps (closely related to sea anemones) are the master engineers. Forming colonies linked by a network of tubes and protected by an external skeleton of lime, they forever grow upon the mass remains of their forebears. Their formations are as varied in color as in shape, from red fans to yellow staghorn, purple "brains" to green cabbage, and many, many more.

Snorkeling or diving in the reef is like taking a swim through an underwater garden. I've put on a mask and fins in bodies of water all over the world, from Hawaii to the Indian Ocean, but never have I been more astounded than on the Barrier Reef.

More than 1,400 species of fish have been identified here, each seemingly brighter and more fanciful than the next. There are turtles and rays, starfish and sea urchins, jellyfish and giant clams, and more.

The polyps' only known enemy, by the way—besides the polluting or vandalizing human—is the crown-of-thorns star-fish. This creature is a formidable foe indeed, one posing a real challenge to marine biologists trying to control the escalating degeneration of parts of the reef.

The best place from which to approach the underwater won-derland of the Great Barrier reef is right where you are now. At its southern end, the reef is nearly 160 km (100 miles) from the Queensland coast near Rockhampton, and it takes a long boat trip (or a seaplane hop) to reach it. From Cairns, it's but a 20- to 30-km (12- to 20-mile) trip from the Australian mainland to the inner edge of the reef.

▲▲ **Michaelmas Cay**, 45 km (28 miles) northeast of Cairns, is of particular note among the reef islets because it is a tern rook-ery. Thousands of the squawking seabirds circle overhead, pro-tecting their young in their nests and squabbling over shellfish on the isle's sands. (Visitors may carry umbrellas to protect themselves from smelly aerial assaults.) The cay also has superb diving on the offshore reef.

A Hayles' Cruises launch leaves the Green Island Jetty daily at 8:30 a.m., stops at Green Island for two hours, then continues to Michaelmas Cay. A buffet lunch, snorkeling gear, and rides on a submarinelike reef viewer are provided free to all who pay the A$54 fare.

▲▲▲ **Hastings Reef** lies on the reef's outer fringe, where the coral is the youngest and the variety and color of marine life is the greatest. Don't let cloudy weather put you off a trip to this submarine phenomenon, 55 km (34 miles) northeast of Cairns. For one thing, you might not burn as quickly in the less-than-sunny skies. For another, the filtration of rays through the clouds actually brings out the reef's colors better, especially the blues.

Hayles' Outer Barrier Reef cruise leaves Cairns at 8:30 a.m. daily, stops for two hours at Green Island (where it is joined by Green Island overnighters), does a slow circle around Michaelmas Cay, then anchors at Hastings Reef for three hours. An all-inclusive fare of A$65 includes a buffet lunch, morning and afternoon tea, snorkeling gear (and instruction from a professional dive team), rides on the Reef Pioneer subsea coral viewer, and video films of reef life. Scuba-diving equipment can be rented by qualified divers.

CAIRNS TO BRISBANE

The scenic Kuranda Railway will take you inland to the edge of the rain-forested Atherton Tableland, climbing steeply above fields of sugarcane to the Barron River Gorge. In Kuranda, you'll have time to see Barron Falls, the open-air market, and the Noctarium before returning to Cairns after lunch. Take a late afternoon flight to Brisbane.

Suggested Schedule

7:30	Breakfast at hotel; store your packed bags.
9:00*	Depart Cairns by rail for Kuranda.
10:30	Arrive Kuranda. Browse through the market, with plenty of time left to see sights of your choice and eat a bite of lunch.
1:30*	Depart Kuranda for Cairns.
3:00	Arrive Cairns. Return to your hotel, pick up your bags and head for the airport.
5:15	Depart Cairns on Ansett Flight 39 to Brisbane. Dinner en route.
7:50	Arrive Brisbane. Check into hotel.

    * Cairns-Kuranda schedule may vary slightly by season.

Sightseeing Highlights

▲▲▲The Cairns-Kuranda Railway was an engineering marvel of the late 1800s. Between 1886 and 1891, a team of more than 1,500 laborers carved this 34-km (21-mile) narrow-gauge track from the side of a mountain using pick, shovel, and dynamite. They installed 15 tunnels, 98 curves, and dozens of bridges in the 1,055-foot climb from lush canefields up the Barron River Gorge to Kuranda village on the edge of the Atherton Tableland.

Today, tourists can make the same dramatic journey in colonial-style railcars for a round-trip price of A$18-$25. After leaving Cairns (or the alternate restaurant-depot in suburban Freshwater), the train climbs past Horseshoe Bend, with vast views across the checkerboard of canefields to the Coral Sea. (On clear days, you can easily pick out Green Island on the Great Barrier Reef.) After passing Stony Creek Falls, there are breathtaking views of the precipitous Barron River Gorge wherever breaks in the dense rain forest vegetation allow. The train finally emerges at the great Barron Falls, a short distance from Kuranda.

▲**Barron Falls** must have been magnificent before its power-ful waters were harnessed by a major hydroelectric project. A small quantity of water is still allowed to trickle over the huge rock wall—more, of course, during rainy season—to allow visi-tors to imagine the former grandeur of this great cataract. The train makes a photo stop at the Falls Lookout at the end of the Barron Falls Road from Kuranda. There's also a track from the lookout to the bottom of the gorge for hiking diehards.

▲**Kuranda Railway Station** is a lovely relic of bygone days. Built in 1915, it is an oasis in the midst of a tropical jungle and is itself a greenhouse of hanging ferns.

▲**Kuranda** (pop. 500) lives up to its billing as "the village in the rain forest." Its tree-lined main street, which leads about a half-mile from the station to the market, features numerous arts and crafts galleries and Devonshire tea shops. Horse-drawn carts travel the short route.

Wednesday and Sunday are market days in Kuranda. The open-air **Kuranda Market**, winding around a hill and across a small stream at the west end of town, gives local artisans and fruit growers a chance to sell their wards and produce. Here's where you'll find hand-painted T-shirts, leather goods, pottery and woodwork, as well as tropical delights like mangoes, starfruit, and custard apples. The market is open rain or shine, April to October, Wednesdays 9:00 a.m. to noon and Sundays 9:00 a.m. to 1:00 p.m. Nearby is the small **Heritage Home-stead** historical museum (admission A$3).

Across the road from the market is the **Kuranda Wildlife Noctarium**, an indoor zoo with simulated forest conditions for nocturnal Australian fauna (admission A$4.50). Also in Kuranda, you'll find the **Honey House**, where bees in glass hives pro-duce honey sold behind the counter (free admission); the **Cape York Experience**, an audiovisual program screening daily at Kurunda Village Centre (admission A$3.50); and the **Jilli Binna Museum**, a display of artifacts from Aboriginal rain forest cul-ture (admission A50 cents). The **Australian Butterfly Farm**, just out of town, is a major new attraction. Back near the rail-way station, the *Kurunda Queen* departs hourly for a 50-minute riverboat cruise on the Barron River (fare A$6.50).

Brisbane Orientation

It has only been in recent years that Brisbane has begun to out-grow its reputation as a "big country town" and develop a bit of sophistication. Now that it has tasted the cultured life, though, it shows no signs of backing off.

Queensland's capital, a city of 1.1 million people, sprawls for an amazing 471 square miles around both banks of the Brisbane River. (That makes it the third-largest city in the world in area.) Its downtown core, however, is relatively small, swallowing up a single horseshoe bend some 30 km upriver from Moreton Bay.

Like several other Australian cities, Brisbane (pronounced "Briz-b'n") got its start as a convict settlement. British Lieutenant John Oxley founded the colony in 1824. Agricultural and mining wealth from the vast inland reaches of the state made the city prosperous in the late nineteenth and early twentieth centuries. Today, behind (some say in spite of) the leadership of Queensland's controversial, ultraconservative, 79-year-old premier, Joh Bjelke-Petersen (you'll hear his name mentioned often), Brisbane has blossomed into a progressive garden city.

The symbol of this newfound refinement is the Queensland Cultural Centre, a brilliant fine and performing arts complex on the banks of the river, across from downtown. It adjoins the riverfront site of World Expo '88, an international exposition in the mold of Vancouver's Expo '86, which ran from April 30 to October 30, 1988.

Brisbane has a subtropical climate, with warm, rainy summers (temperatures range from 67 to 85 degrees F) and drier winters (49 to 69 degrees F).

Most of the main streets in downtown Brisbane have been named after British rulers, so if you know your English history, this should come easy. From the direction of the airport, in northeast Brisbane, Ann Street is the principal thoroughfare leading into downtown. It skirts the central railway station and King George Square, essentially marking the northwestern edge of the city center. Albert Street, running at right angles to Ann Street through the square, is the main northwest-southeast artery. Ann is paralleled to the southeast by Adelaide, Queen, Elizabeth, Charlotte, Mary, Margaret, and Alice streets, with the Botanic Gardens taking the southernmost chunk of the "horse-shoe." Albert is paralleled to the southwest by George and William streets, and to the northeast by Edward, Creek, and Wharf streets. King George Square, on which sits the City Hall, and Queen Street between Albert and Edward are pedestrian malls.

City Transportation
Skennars Transport (tel. 832-1148) provides shuttle-bus service to downtown Brisbane from the domestic and international airport terminals, a distance of some 10 km (6 miles). Buses run half-hourly, and the charge is A$2.70. (You can also catch a No. 160 city bus for A80 cents.) Taxis charge about A$7 over the same distance. Several car rental agencies have desks at the airport, but you probably won't need one for the remainder of your stay.

Within the city, Queensland Railways' electric Citytrain (tel. 225-0211) and City Council buses (tel. 225-4444) provide service to nearly all points. Six Citytrain lines extend some 45 km (28 miles) east-west from Shorncliffe to Ipswich, 75 km (45 miles) north-south from Caboolture to Beenleigh. Trains operate daily from approximately 4:30 a.m. to 1:30 a.m. (with limited hours on weekends). A one-segment fare is A60 cents. Bus tickets are A50 cents for one zone, A80 cents for two, or you can buy a A$3 Day Rover ticket providing unlimited bus transport for one day (5:30 a.m. to 11:30 p.m.). There's also a Brisbane River Ferry Service (tel. 399-4768) providing river crossings at several points for just A40 cents. Brisbane Bicycle Hire, 214 Margaret St. (tel. 229-2592), has bicycles for rent at A$3.50 an hour or A$12 an 8-hour day.

Where to Stay

Brisbane is among the more expensive Australian cities for overnight stays, and it's not getting any cheaper. Its two newest
hotels—the **Hilton International**, 190 Elizabeth St. (tel.
231-3131), and the **Sheraton Brisbane**, 249 Turbot St. (tel.
835-3535)—are luxury, world-class accommodations. The Hilton features a 25-story garden atrium, while the 441-room Sheraton looms directly above the central station. A small step down
in price is the **Mayfair Crest**, a businessmen's favorite at Ann
and Roma streets, King George Square (tel. 229-9111).

The **Brisbane City Travelodge**, Roma Street near George
Street (tel. 238-2222), is one of Brisbane's best bargains, with
luxury-class facilities at moderate prices. Also centrally located
and midpriced are the **Bellevue Hotel**, 103 George St. (tel.
221-6044); the **Parkview Motel**, 128 Alice St. (tel. 31-2695);
and the **Regal Motel**, 132 Alice St. (tel. 31-1541).

The **Yale Budget Inn**, 413 Upper Edward St. (tel. 832-1663),
is a bed-and-breakfast guest house extremely popular among
economy travelers. **Marrs Town House**, 391 Wickham Terrace
(tel. 831-5388), is a newer accommodation near Albert Park,
while the **Atcherly Hotel**, 513 Queen St. (tel. 832-2591), is an
old standby.

Budget travelers must book at the downtown YHA office, 462
Queen St., before catching a No. 172 bus north to the **Brisbane
Youth Hostel**, 15 Mitchell St. in Kedron (tel. 57-1245), 8 km
north of the city center. Much nearer town are the two indepen-
dent **Brisbane Backpackers Inns** in New Farm, at 71 Kent St.
(tel. 385-4504) and 365 Bowen Terrace (tel. 358-1488).

Where to Eat

No one is accusing Brisbane of being the gastronomic capital of
Australia. But there are a number of good restaurants, as befits a
city of this size.

The southeast Queensland coast is reknowned for its
seafood—particularly the Moreton Bay bugs (a lobster relation)
and the Queensland mud crabs. You can't go wrong ordering
them at **Gambaro's**, a casual café just west of downtown at 34
Caxton St., Petrie Terrace, or the **Breakfast Creek Wharf**, east
of the central city at 160 Breakfast Creek Road, Newstead.
Downtown, **Conia's**, 132 Albert St., has excellent seafood.

In the central city area, the best upmarket dining is in the best
hotels. **Michael's Riverside**, in the new Riverside Centre at
123 Eagle St., wins plaudits for its highbrow French cuisine. But
many casual, less expensive spots are fun, too—like **Jimmy's
on the Mall**, a licensed, open-air restaurant in the Queen Street

Mall. In the Elizabeth Arcade off Charlotte Street, **Tortilla** (Aussies pronounce the "L"'s) is an atmospheric choice for decent Mexican food and **The Source** has good, cheap vegetarian offerings. **Mama Luigi's**, 240 St. Paul's Terrace, is a longtime Italian favorite, and you can eat like a Russian at **Czars**, 47 Elizabeth St.

The adjacent suburbs of Fortitude Valley and New Farm, walking distance east of downtown (via Ann or Wickham St.), feature many authentic, low-priced ethnic restaurants. Try **Giardinetto's** (Italian), 336 Brunswick St.; **Cathay** (Chinese), 222 Wickham St.; **Baan Thai** (Thai), 630 Brunswick St.; and **Possum's** (fair dinkum Aussie), 681 Brunswick St. Farther toward the airport, the **Breakfast Creek Hotel**, 2 Kingsford Smith Drive, has a nationally famous steak-and-beer garden.

In Petrie Terrace, **Rag's**, 25 Caxton St., has a reputation as Brisbane's best French restaurant. The **Caxton Garden Grill**, in the Caxton Hotel, provides jazz accompaniment to meals. In nearby Paddington, the **Elephant Bath**, 183 Given Terrace, offers a rare Asian delight: Sri Lankan curries.

Nightlife

The **Performing Arts Complex**, in the aforementioned Queensland Cultural Centre, contains the Concert Hall for symphonic performances, the Lyric Theatre for opera, ballet, drama, and musical comedy, and the Cremorne Theatre for smaller and experimental productions. Almost any major performance will be presented here. Events schedule can be obtained and bookings made by calling 844-0201 or visiting the PAC box office. The Cultural Centre is on the south side of the Brisbane River at Grey and Melbourne streets.

Other good spots for live theater include the **S.G.I.O. Theatre**, Turbot and Albert streets, home of the Queensland Theatre Company, and **La Boite**, 57 Hale St. in Milton, home of the Brisbane Repertory Company. Queensland film censors are more protective of viewers than other states, but you'll find a good number of movie theaters in the downtown area, especially on Albert Street.

Brisbane's most popular disco-nightclubs, at this writing, were **Sibyl's**, 383 Adelaide St., with three floors of dancing and entertainment; and the **Brisbane Underground**, Caxton and Hal streets in Paddington. Both are open until 3:00 a.m. Wednesdays through Saturdays. The major hotels all have their posh night spots.

For live music, try the **Hacienda Hotel**, Brunswick and McLachlan streets in Fortitude Valley, for rock; the **Blue Moon Cafe**, 540 Queen St., for jazz; or the **Treasury Hotel**, Elizabeth and George streets, for blues. **Wilson's 1870**, 103 Queen St., appeals to an older crowd with a piano bar and cocktail music.

Helpful Hints

The **Brisbane Visitors and Convention Bureau** (tel. 221-8411), in City Hall on the west side of King George Square, is open weekdays 8:30 a.m. to 5:00 p.m. **The Queensland Government Travel Centre** is at 196 Adelaide St. (tel. 31-2211), open 9:00 a.m. to 4:45 p.m. Monday to Friday, 9:00 to 11:15 a.m. Saturday. There are tourist information booths in the Queen Street Mall and the Brisbane Transit Centre on Roma Street.

The **General Post Office** on Queen Street is open Monday to Friday, 7:00 a.m. to 7:00 p.m. Banking hours are 9:30 a.m. to 4:00 p.m. Monday to Thursday, to 5:00 p.m. Friday. Retail shops in the central city are open 8:15 a.m. to 5:00 p.m. Monday to Thursday, to 9:00 p.m. Friday, to noon Saturday. It's hard to find anything open on a Sunday.

There's an **American Consulate** at 383 Wickham Terrace (tel. 839-8955). In case of emergencies, dial 000. There's also a 24-hour number for medical service: 378-6900.

BRISBANE AND THE GOLD COAST

Your time is limited, so it's a good day to see the sights from a city tour bus. Be sure the itinerary includes the Lone Pine Koala Sanctuary: if you ever wanted a photo of yourself holding one of these seemingly cuddly creatures, here's where to have it taken. After lunch, take a bus to the Gold Coast, Australia's answer to Miami Beach. Catch the day's last rays on the beach.

Suggested Schedule

8:00	Breakfast at hotel.
9:00	Half-day morning tour of city, including the Lone Pine Koala Sanctuary, Mount Coot-tha Gardens and the Queensland Cultural Centre.
12:30	Return from tour. Lunch.
2:00	Board a bus for the Gold Coast.
3:30	Arrive at Surfers Paradise. Check into hotel.
4:30	Hit the beach.
6:30	Relax at hotel.
7:30	Dinner.
9:00	Rage.

Brisbane Sightseeing Highlights

▲▲ **City tours** are something I'm not normally crazy about— mainly because I prefer to explore a new place on my own time—but given the limited time allotted to Brisbane in this itinerary, a bus tour is the most efficient way to see the main attractions. Ansett Pioneer Tours (tel. 226-1184) show off the city sights in a half-day tour leaving major hotels at 9:00 a.m. daily (fare A$12); Aladdin's Magic Carpet Tours (tel. 345-8300) start just 15 minutes later (fare A$14). Both "Beautiful Brisbane" tours last 3½ hours. Boomerang Tours' (tel. 221-9922) three-hour "Morning City Sights" tour (fare A$10) starts at 10:00 a.m. Saturday, Sunday, and Monday only.

▲▲▲ **Lone Pine Koala Sanctuary**, on the banks of the Brisbane River off Jesmond Road in Fig Tree Pocket, 11 km (7 miles) from the city center, has more koalas (over 100) than any other wildlife reserve in Australia. You can have your photo taken cuddling one of the creatures (beware the sharp claws), visit the maternity wing and see newborn koalas, and feed the freely roaming kangaroos and emus. There are a variety of other Australian animals, birds, and reptiles in the park as well. Open daily 9:30 a.m. to 5:00 p.m. Adult admission is A$6.50.

You can reach the Lone Pine Sanctuary on your own by taking a No. 84 bus from Adelaide Street. A better way to arrive, if you've got an afternoon free, is to join the Koala Cruise (tel. 229-7055) leaving daily at 1:15 p.m. from Queens Wharf Road, North Quay (near downtown). The cruise costs A$9; combined with a return coach tour, it's A$14.

▲**Mount Coot-tha Botanic Gardens**, Toowong, feature native and imported plants in the tropical rain forest, subtropical, and desert settings. They're open daily 7:00 a.m. to 5:00 p.m. The Sir Thomas Brisbane Planetarium offers a stargazing show from Wednesday to Sunday between noon and 7:00 p.m.; bookings are essential. Atop Mount Coot-tha, just 8 km (5 miles) from the city center, is a restaurant with panoramic views all the way to Moreton Bay. Other major gardens in Brisbane include the City Botanic Gardens at the south end of Albert Street; New Farm Park, east of downtown off Brunswick Street; and Newstead Park on Breakfast Creek Road, harboring Brisbane's oldest building, the 1846 Newstead House.

▲▲**The Queensland Cultural Centre** occupies a 14.7-acre site on the south bank of the Brisbane River, facing the city center across the Victoria Bridge. A series of distinctive white structures set amid landscaped gardens, sculptures, and water malls, this A$173 million complex has four components: the Queensland Art Gallery (opened in 1982), the Performing Arts Complex (1985), the Queensland Museum (1986), and the State Library (1988). A convention center, three restaurants, four cafeterias, and several specialty shops are among its facilities. The Queensland Cultural Centre Trust (tel. 240-7229) has full information.

The Queensland Art Gallery (tel. 240-7333) displays its permanent collection of Australian and European art, plus numerous touring shows, in 15 separate exhibition areas. A wide variety of lectures, workshops, and musical performances are regularly offered. There's free admission to the gallery, open daily 10:00 a.m. to 5:00 p.m., Wednesday to 8:00 p.m. Guided tours are available weekdays at 11:00 a.m., 1:00 p.m., and 2:00 p.m., and weekends at 2:00 and 3:00 p.m., for no additional charge. The 124-year-old **Queensland Museum** (tel. 240-7633) has three floors of displays emphasizing the state's geology and natural history, Aboriginal roots and Melanesian influences, pioneer history, and early technology. Popular with children is a large outdoor Dinosaur Garden. Open daily 9:00 a.m. to 5:00 p.m., Wednesday to 8:00 p.m. Admission is free.

The Performing Arts Complex (tel. 240-7483) attracted nearly 1 million patrons to its three theaters during its first two years of operation (see "Nightlife," Day 19). Performers included the Royal Shakespeare Company, the Bolshoi Ballet, and the London Philharmonic Orchestra. Guided tours are offered hourly, 10:00 a.m. to 4:00 p.m., Monday to Saturday, for A$2.50. There are backstage tours on selected days by reservation for A$5.

▲ **The Australian Woolshed**, 15 km (9½ miles) from downtown at 148 Samford Road, Ferny Hills, is as close as you're likely to get to an authentic Aussie sheep station in a metropolitan area. Working sheepdogs demonstrate their skill, and there are exhibits of wool classing and spinning. There's no admission charge to the complex, open daily 9:30 a.m. to 6:00 p.m., but if you want to see the shearing demonstration and parade of trained rams at 10:45 a.m. daily or 2:00 p.m. Sunday, you'll have to pay A$4.50. The craft shop has been voted Australia's best. A licensed outback-style restaurant features "bush dances" on Friday and Saturday from 7:00 p.m. to midnight.

▲ **Earlystreet Historical Village**, 75 McIlwraith Ave., Norman Park, is a collection of eight historic Queensland buildings set in five acres of colonial gardens surrounding the nineteenth-century Eulalia Manor. You'll find an old slab hut, a shearers' pub, a general store, a blacksmith's shop, a coach house, and several residences, all relocated to this site and refurnished in mid-1800s style. Classified by the National Trust, the village is open weekdays 9:30 a.m. to 4:30 p.m., Saturday and Sunday from 10:30 a.m. Admission is A$4.

▲ **The Kookaburra Queen** is an elegant wooden paddle wheeler that cruises the waters of the Brisbane River several times daily. Ninety-minute tea or snack cruises, leaving at 10:00 a.m. (daily except Saturday), 12:45 p.m. (weekdays), and 3:00 p.m. (Sundays), cost just A$10.90. Daily dinner cruises, boarding at 7:00 p.m., are priced from A$27.90 to A$34.90. The Queen leaves from the Petrie Bight Marina on Howard Street, at the east end of the city near the National Hotel.

The Paddington Circle is the quaintest shopping area in Brisbane. Merchants have retained and restored the suburb's original colonial architecture to give the entire district a heritage feeling. Most of the shops are along Given Terrace and Latrobe Terrace.

World Expo '88

From April 30 to October 30, 1988, Brisbane hosted the single largest event in Australian history, the first international exposition to be held in the Southern Hemisphere since the Melbourne World's Fair of 1888. With a theme of "Leisure in the Age of Technology," some 30 countries and an equal number of corporations took part in the fair, which attracted more than 10 million visitors from throughout Australia and overseas. The

99-acre Expo site spreads for a full kilometer along the south bank of the Brisbane River beside the new Queensland Cultural Centre. In 1989, a five-year, A$1 billion redevelopment project was launched. Park areas, entertainment facilities, and indoor and outdoor eating spots are projected.

Getting to the Gold Coast

Except in the middle of the night, you'll never have to wait longer than an hour or two to catch a bus from Brisbane to Australia's favorite beach resort. Greyhound buses (tel. 240-9333) leave at least 10 times a day from the Roma Street Transit Centre. The buses of Skennars Transport (tel. 38-9444 in Surfers, 36-2574 in Coolangatta) offer direct shuttle service from the Gold Coast to Brisbane International Airport. The fare is A$8.10. Remember to allow 1 ½ hours for the trip from Surfers, two hours from Coolangatta.

There's talk of opening a rail link between Brisbane and the Gold Coast, but at this writing it's still at least a year from completion.

Gold Coast Orientation

A glittering white-sand beach stretching 32 km (20 miles) down the coast of southeasternmost Queensland, just 65 km (40 miles) from Brisbane, the Gold Coast is the single most popular resort strip in Australia. That has both good and bad connotations. There are hotels, restaurants, and night spots of all standards and prices, a lush mountain backdrop not far from the lovely beach, and an incredible variety of man-made attractions. But there's also a great deal of crass commercialism and tourist kitsch preying on the throngs in transition. Overlook that and you'll have a great time.

At least a dozen separate communities, linked by the busy Gold Coast Highway, comprise the city of Gold Coast. About 200,000 people make their home along this narrow strip, four times the population of 20 years ago. Southport, the Gold Coast's northernmost community, is its commercial and industrial center. Surfers Paradise, the next main center reached heading south, is the Waikiki-style high-rise capital of the coast and the site of its most frenetic nightlife. Halfway down the coast is Burleigh Heads, a laid-back family community at the foot of fauna-rich Burleigh Heads National Park. Coolangatta marks not only the southern extreme of the Gold Coast but also the boundary between Queensland and New South Wales. The Gold Coast Airport, with direct links to Sydney, Melbourne, Adelaide, and other cities, is here.

Local Transportation

Don't worry about being stuck on the Gold Coast without a car. You can either base yourself in one town and cope quite nicely or you can call upon Surfside buses (tel. 36-2449) for regular transportation links between Southport and Coolangatta. No fare is higher than A$2. Smekels Busline (tel. 32-6211) serves the Southport area more thoroughly but doesn't go farther south than Broadbeach. Silly Style, 6 Beach Road, Surfers, will rent you a bike or moped.

Where to Stay

As Surfers Paradise (usually called "Surfers") is the center of most of the action, we'll deal with it first. At the top of the line are the elegant **Ramada At Paradise Center**, Gold Coast Highway and Hanlan Street (tel. 075/59-3400), and the **Holiday Inn-Surfers Paradise**, 22 View St. (tel. 59-1000). The **Chevron Paradise Hotel**, Ferny Avenue (tel. 39-0444), is a good choice in the moderate price bracket. You're reaching a bit to find a decent economy room in Surfers, but the **Hub Motel**, 21 Cavill Ave. (tel. 31-5559), will do quite nicely. The nearest budget accommodation to Surfers is the AYH hostel in the **El Dorado Motel**, 2821 Gold Coast Highway (tel. 31-5155), nearly a mile south of Surfers. You must check in between 4:00 and 6:00 p.m.

Outside of Surfers, the best accommodation is the **Conrad International Hotel**, Gold Coast Highway, Broadbeach Island (tel. 92-1133). It's the site of Jupiter's Casino. You'll find moderate- and economy-priced motels all along the Gold Coast Highway from here south, but Coolangatta is the king in these price ranges. Try the **Pacific Village Hotel**, 88 Marine Parade (tel. 36-2733), or the **Bombora Holiday Lodge**, Marine Parade at Dutton Street (tel. 36-1888). The **Backpackers Inn**, 45 McLean St., Coolangatta (tel. 36-2422), costs less than A$8 a night and has a licensed restaurant and bar on the premises.

Where to Eat

There are as many different kinds of places to eat on the Gold Coast as there are kinds of people who visit, and that's a lot. The coast's characterization as a utopia for junk-food junkies is not totally inaccurate, but there is no shortage of more wholesome dining establishments.

In Surfers, try the **Rusty Pelican**, Orchid and Elkhorn avenues, or the **Captain's Tale**, 5 Cavill Ave. on the mall, for seafood; **Pellegrini**, 3120 Gold Coast Highway, for Italian cuisine; or **Shogun**, 90 Bundall Road, for Japanese food. Be

warned, however: none of them are cheap. You can spend less money and have a lot of fun at the hofbrau-style **Bavarian Steak House**, Gold Coast Highway at Cavill Avenue; the **Tandoori Taj** (North Indian), 3100 Gold Coast Highway; the **Mexican Kitchen**, 150 Bundall Road; or the **Athens** (Greek), Gold Coast Highway near Laycock Street. The **Surfer's Deli**, 25 Orchid Avenue, is a pleasant sidewalk café with light meals and entertainment.

Up and down the coast the **Holy Mackerel**, 174 Marine Parade, Labrador (north of Southport), offers free shuttle service from Surfers to its seafood restaurant. Mermaid Beach has a good Italian restaurant, **Gino's Osteria**, 2563 Gold Coast Highway, and nearby on the same road, the most passionately named vegetarian eatery I've ever heard of—the **Lusty Lentil**.

Farther down, in Burleigh Heads, the **Chieng Mai Thai** restaurant is at 31 James St. Finally, no south end budget watcher should pass up a A$3.30 counter meal at the **Queensland Hotel**, Boundary Street, Coolangatta.

Nightlife

The cards are dealt 24 hours a day at **Jupiter's Casino** in the Conrad International Hotel on Broadbeach Island. Blackjack, roulette, craps, baccarat, keno, and several other games are played continuously in this sophisticated new casino. There are also several restaurants and a showroom featuring world-class entertainers.

In Surfers, the overloaded disco-cabaret lineup includes such standouts as **Twains International** and the five-story **Penthouse**, both on Orchid Avenue. The **Swingin' Vine**, 47A Cavill Ave., is noted for jazz and comedy. Ask for directions to **Bombay Rock**, the best of several clubs in Surfers that feature live rock. Its counterpart, 13 km (8 miles) south of Surfers in North Palm Beach, is the **Playroom**, on the Gold Coast Highway opposite the Tallebudgera Bridge.

There's cheaper entertainment just across the New South Wales border from Coolangatta in the town of Tweed Heads. The club scene flourishes here where poker machines ("one-armed bandits") are legal. Meals, drinks, and top-flight entertainment are always reduced in price to entice you to play the polies. They're technically membership clubs, but out-of-state visitors, especially foreigners, are welcomed. Shuttle buses can run you from Surfers or elsewhere on the Gold Coast to such spots as **Twin Towns Services Club**, Wharf Street; **Tweed Heads Bowls Club**, Tweed Street; and my favorite, **Seagulls Rugby League Football Club**, Gollan Drive.

For romancers or real budget watchers, there's nothing cheaper than a walk on a moonlit beach.

Helpful Hints

The Gold Coast Visitors and Convention Bureau has its main offices in the Cavill Mall, Surfers Paradise (tel. 38-4419). (There's a Coolangatta branch: tel. 26-7765.) You'll also find the Queensland Government Travel Centre here on the second floor of the TAA Building, 38-40 Cavill Ave. (tel. 92-1033). All are open 9:00 a.m. to 4:45 p.m. weekdays, 9:00 to 11:15 a.m. Saturday.

The Surfers Paradise post office is at the corner of Cavill Avenue and the Gold Coast Highway. Banking hours are 9:30 a.m. to 4:00 p.m. Monday to Thursday, to 5:00 p.m. Friday. Retail shops are open daily except Sunday, 9:00 a.m. to 5:30 p.m.

In case of emergencies, dial 000. For 24-hour medical assistance, call 38-8823.

THE GOLD COAST

Your final day on Australian beaches. Why not decide for yourself if the name "Surfers Paradise" really fits? Or dive into a grab
bag of tourist attractions such as Sea World, the Currumbin Bird
Sanctuary, or the Mudgeeraba Boomerang Farm.

Suggested Schedule	
7:30	Up and at 'em, unless you need extra sleep to recover from last night's fling.
9:00	Visit the Currumbin Bird Sanctuary near Palm Beach.
11:00	Catch a few late morning rays.
12:30	Lunch.
1:30	Sea World is worth a full afternoon.
5:00	Head back to your hotel. Take a quick dip in the pool.
6:30	Dinner.
8:00	It's your last night in Australia—what you do with it is up to you.

Sightseeing Highlights
▲▲The Currumbin Bird Sanctuary, just off the Gold Coast
Highway on Tomewin Street, Currumbin, 18 km (11 miles) south
of Surfers, is a tourist favorite mainly because of the flocks of
brightly colored rainbow lorikeets that fly in daily from their
homes in the wild to be fed from plates of honey by willing visitors. Arrive before 10:00 a.m. to see the mass of orange-
breasted, blue-headed, green-backed birds, or wait until about
4:00 in the afternoon. A variety of other native birds, koalas,
kangaroos, and wallabies make their homes in the 50-acre wildlife refuge. You can walk among the critters or watch from a
2-km miniature railway. Numerous craftsmen ply their trades;
among them are potters, glassblowers, and gem cutters. Open
daily 8:00 a.m. to 5:00 p.m. Adult admission is A$8.
▲▲Sea World, on the Spit 5 km (3 miles) north of Surfers, is
Australia's No. 1 marine theme park. Dolphins, killer whales,
and sea lions alternately awe and amuse audiences in separate
shows, as do acrobatic water skiers. The World of the Sea Theatre combines audiovisuals with live demonstrations of underwater diving and shark feeding. Visitors can pet dolphins, feed

sea lions, and gaze at an enormous aquarium. The park's dozen rides include Australia's first free-fall waterslide (with a frightening five-story drop!) and its only triple-loop roller coaster, as well as a monorail and carousel for those with less intestinal fortitude.

Sea World is open daily (except Christmas) from 10:00 a.m. to 5:00 p.m. The adult admission of A$18 includes all rides and performances. Call 32-1055 or 32-5131 (recorded) for daily show times and bus connections.

Dreamworld, in Coomera 15 minutes toward Brisbane from Surfers, is Australia's largest Disney-style theme park. This 208-acre complex has a little of everything, some of which will remind you very much of parks in Anaheim and Orlando. You can see the Koala Country Music Show, for example, with 22 life-size but computerized Aussie animals doing the singing and playing. You can take any of 17 different rides, among them a steam train, a "Murrissippi River" cruise, and a high-speed trip through Avalanche Mountain. Sound familiar? Seventeen shops and 11 restaurants take care of shopping and hunger pangs.

Dreamworld is open Saturday to Wednesday, 10:00 a.m. to 5:00 p.m., daily during school holiday periods. Adult admission of A$15 includes all rides and performances. Round-trip express bus service from the Gold Coast is offered for A$6 by Keith's Tours (tel. 30-5908).

Magic Mountain, on the Gold Coast Highway at Nobby's Beach near Miami, is another man-made attraction of the same ilk. You can't miss seeing the medieval castle atop the bluff long before you arrive. The numerous rides include a chair lift to carry you to the mountaintop for panoramic views of the Gold Coast. But the highlight of a visit is "Visions," a superb show presented by magician and illusionist Arthur Coghlan. Open Sunday to Thursday, 10:00 a.m. to 5:00 p.m., daily in summer and during school holiday periods. Adult admission of A$10.50 includes all rides and shows. Call 52-2333 to arrange free bus pickup from hotels.

Burleigh Heads National Park is a small, unexpected natural bushland oasis in the middle of this utterly commercial strip. Koalas, wallabies, bandicoots, and much birdlife inhabit this bluff overlooking the mouth of Tallebudgera Creek. A graded 3-km (2-mile) walking track leads around the headland.

Mudgeeraba Boomerang Farm, on Springbrook Road 20 minutes inland from the Gold Coast, is not a major tourist attraction. Unlike others, however, it's uniquely Australian. Not only will the Hawes family sell you a boomerang made in their own factory but they'll also teach you how to throw it so that it comes back to you. Their 200-acre farm also has a fascinating boomerang museum. Open seven days a week. Ask directions locally or phone 30-5231.

▲**Lamington National Park** comprises some 50,000 acres of lushly forested mountains 43 km (27 miles) from the Gold Coast via Nerang. Some call it "the Green behind the Gold." The park contains 140 km (87 miles) of walking tracks, an estimated 500 waterfalls, and a forest of 3,000-year-old beech trees. Two small guest houses, at Binna Burra and O'Reilly's, serve park visitors.

Grundy's at Paradise Centre is the sort of place that shoppers and fun-seekers don't need to be told about: they'll find it on their own. Set dead center in Surfers Paradise, with direct access from the beach, Ramada Hotel, or Cavill Mall, this three-story complex includes 110 boutiques and specialty shops, an international food village and the most cacophonous collection of video games you've ever heard (or seen).

Pacific Fair, near the casino-hotel in Broadbeach, is the Gold Coast's other most interesting shopping center. The architects have re-created streets from all over the world—from Oxford Street (London) to the Boulevard St. Michel (Paris), Basin Street (New Orleans) to Lindenstrasse (Berlin). Appropriate specialty shops intermingle with chain department stores.

FLY HOME FROM BRISBANE

It's been a great 22 days. Board your flight home to the States in Brisbane this afternoon. Thanks to the International Date Line, you'll reach the U.S. West Coast only 1½ hours after leaving Australia. The longest day of your life was custom-made for savoring those great Australian memories.

Suggested Schedule

8:00	Rise and shine, eat breakfast, and pack everything but your bathing suit.
9:00	You've got three hours left for the beach.
12:00	Grab a Vegemite sandwich for lunch, scoop up your bags, and board a bus for Brisbane airport.
1:30	Arrive at the airport for check-in.
3:00	Qantas Flight 25 leaves for Honolulu, with connections there to San Francisco, Los Angeles, and other cities in the U.S. and Canada.

Farewell Advice

Call your airline first thing in the morning to reconfirm your departure time. Hopefully, you will also have telephoned a couple days earlier from Brisbane to confirm your seat.

The buses of Skennars Transport (tel. 38-9444 in Surfers, 36-2574 in Coolangatta) offer direct shuttle service from the Gold Coast to Brisbane International Airport. The fare is A$8.10. Remember to allow 1½ hours for the trip from Surfers, 2 hours from Coolangatta.

When you reach Brisbane, instruct the driver that you need the international terminal. The domestic terminal, where you arrived, is a considerable drive away, around the runways. Don't spend all your money before reaching the airport. You'll have to hold A$20 out to pay the airport departure tax. As you head back home across the Pacific, you can think back on a great three-week vacation—and where you want to go on your next trip Down Under.

The biggest frustration in trying to cover an entire continent in 22 days is omitting so many worthwhile spots from the itinerary. If you've got the time, the following options can be spliced into your schedule as follows:

Tasmania—Leave from and return to Melbourne (Day 8).
Adelaide and/or Perth—Between Melbourne and Alice Springs (Day 11).
Darwin—Between Alice Springs and Cairns (Day 16).
Great Barrier Reef Islands—Between Cairns and Brisbane (Day 19).

TASMANIA

Australia's island state, some 230 km (143 miles) across Bass Strait from Victoria, is almost a world unto itself. Like a cross between New England and the Pacific Northwest, its colonial manors are scattered through the lowlands beneath forested mountain peaks.

Suggested 6-Day Schedule	
Day 1	Arrive in Devonport from Melbourne. Rent a car and drive to Launceston.
Day 2	See Cataract Gorge, then drive down the east coast via Campbelltown to Point Arthur.
Day 3	After exploring the former penal colony in the morning, drive to Hobart via Richmond.
Day 4	Catch the view from Mount Wellington, then drive via Lake St. Clair and Queenstown to Strahan.
Day 5	Go on the Gordon River cruise in the morning, then drive to Stanley for the night.
Day 6	Putter down the north coast to Devonport. Night flight or ferry voyage back to Melbourne.

Getting There
Two to five flights daily transit the Bass Strait between Melbourne and Hobart (the state capital), Launceston, Devonport, and Burnie/Wynyard. The flight takes 65 minutes to Hobart, 55

minutes to Launceston, 50 minutes to the other two north coast towns. The lowest round-trip fares, at this writing, were A$192 to Hobart, A$165 to Launceston, and A$146 to Devonport and Burnie/Wynyard on a 30-day advance purchase excursion basis. (If you're under 25, **East-West Airlines** will give you a 20% discount.) There are also direct flights several times a week to Launceston and Hobart from Sydney and the Gold Coast.

An overnight ferry, the *Abel Tasman*, crosses the strait three times a week, leaving Melbourne at 6:00 p.m. Monday, Wednesday, and Friday and arriving in Devonport at 8:30 the following morning. Return boats leave Devonport at 6:00 p.m. Tuesday, Thursday, and Sunday. One-way fares vary according to season and facilities but range from A$75 (winter) to A$109 (summer) on the low end to A$141 to A$197 at the high end.

Getting Around

The large auto rental firms—Hertz, Avis, and Budget—are represented in all large towns in Tasmania. Weekly rates, including unlimited kilometers, are similar, ranging from A$282 to A$600 depending upon class of vehicle. You'll get a better deal from **Advance Travel Car Rentals** in Devonport (tel. 004/24-8885) or Launceston (tel. 003/44-2164), with weekly rates starting at A$144.

If you're a solo budget traveler, look into the seven-day "Tassie Pass" with **Tasmanian Redline Coaches** for A$60. (A 14-day pass is only A$75.) Book through Tasbureau (see "Helpful Hints"). The Redline terminal to Devonport is at 9 Edward St. (tel. 004/24-2585); in Launceston at 112 George St. (tel. 003/31-9177); in Hobart at 96 Harrington St. (tel. 004/34-4577).

Sightseeing Highlights

▲**Devonport** (pop. 25,000) is the market center of the fertile north coast region. **Tiagarra**, atop the headland called Mersey Bluff, remembers the culture of the Tasmanian Aboriginal, one of the most tragic races in history. Early settlers hunted down and shot the native Tasmanians until a mere handful survived. They were resettled off Tasmania's north coast, on Flinders Island, where the last one died in 1876. Also in Devonport are the **Don River Railway Museum**, the **Maritime Museum,** and **Taswegia** historic printery and craft gallery.

▲**Launceston** is Tasmania's second city, both in population (65,000) and age (founded in 1805, a year after Hobart). Situated at the head of the tranquil Tamar River, it is noted for its many parks and gardens, especially **Cataract Gorge**. Reminiscent of the Wisconsin Dells, it is surrounded by a rhododendron garden and crossed by an aerial chair lift. Also see the **Queen Victoria Museum and Art Gallery** and the **Waverly Woollen Mills** (tours daily 9:00 a.m. to 4:00 p.m.). Thirteen km (8 miles) west of Launceston, near Hadspen, is the beautiful **Entally House** historic homestead, built in 1819.

▲▲▲**Port Arthur** was a name synonymous with harsh justice in Australia's convict past. Between 1830 and 1877, some 12,500 hardened criminals lived in this isolated location under the threat of the lash and long-term solitary isolation that drove many to madness. Today, the restored **Port Arthur National Historic Site** commemorates the nation's roots like nowhere else.

Elsewhere on the Tasman Peninsula, you can see spectacular coastal formations—arches, undersea caves, and blowholes—that helped make this prison colony so difficult to escape. **The Bush Mill** theme park, 5 km (3 miles) north of the historic site, recalls the days of the early timber cutters. The **Tasmanian**

Devil Park at Taranna, another 5 km north, is a good place to see these varmints.

▲▲ **Richmond** is a detour off the road back to Hobart, just 26 km (16 miles) northeast of the capital. The treasures of this charming 1820s town include Australia's first bridge and its oldest Catholic church. The Richmond Gaol has been faithfully restored. Many of the community's elegant sandstone buildings now house Devonshire tea shops, arts and crafts galleries, and historical museums.

▲▲▲ **Hobart**—Tasmania's capital and largest city (pop. 175,000) was established in 1804 as the second European settlement in Australia. The inner-city suburb of **Battery Point** is the original seamen's quarter, where tiny cottages share the narrow winding streets with Georgian mansions and Victorian terrace houses—now, as often as not, occupied by restaurants, bed-and-breakfasts, art galleries, and antique shops. **The Van Diemen's Land Memorial Folk Museum** in the Narryna mansion at 103 Hampden Road has a superb period collection. The **Maritime Museum of Tasmania** in the Secheron House mansion off Colville Street is also interesting.

Elsewhere in Hobart, see the excellent **Tasmanian Museum and Art Gallery**, the **Royal Tasmanian Botanical Gardens**, and the scale-model **Tudor Court** at Sandy Bay. From the summit of 4,170-foot Mount Wellington, a 20-km (12½-mile) drive from the city center, you can savor the spectacular layout of this beautiful harbor city at the mouth of the Derwent River.

▲▲ **Strahan**, a tiny fishing and timber port, is best known as the starting point for cruises through Macquarie Harbour and up the Gordon River, a crystalline stream that winds through unexplored rain forest from **South West National Park**. Mount Everest conqueror Sir Edmund Hillary has called this region "the greatest walking country in the world." Some believe its denizens may include the legendary Tasmanian wolf, a striped marsupial canine last confirmed alive in the 1930s.

▲ **Stanley** has changed little since it was established in 1826 by sheep breeders. Its combination of history and maritime beauty is accented by **The Nut**, a striking 500-foot mesalike basalt outcropping that dominates coastal scenery for many miles around.

▲ **The Northwest Coast** drive, 129 km (80 miles) along the Bass Highway from Stanley to Devonport, provides a final day of Tasmanian wanderings. **Rocky Cape National Park** contains Aboriginal caves, fields of wild orchids, and the glistening white sand **Sisters Beach** with Birdland Native Gardens reserve. **Lapoinya** rhododendron gardens are nearby. At **Wynyard**, you'll find **Fossil Bluff**, where the oldest marsupial fossil in Australia was discovered. **Burnie** (pop. 21,000) has a major timber products industry and the **Pioneer Village Museum**, re-creating the town's turn-of-the-century commercial center. Proceed east to the town of **Penguin**, which takes its name from colonies of fairy penguins living along the shore; **Ulverstone**, gateway to the Leven Canyon; and finally to **Devonport** and the Abel Tasman ferry terminal.

Helpful Hints

Tasmania calls its state tourist agency **Tasbureau**. The head office is at 80 Elizabeth St., Hobart (tel. 002-30-0211), but you'll find other offices along the route in Devonport (18 Rooke St., tel. 004/24-1526); Launceston (St. John and Paterson streets, tel. 003/32-2101); Queenstown (39 Orr St., tel. 004/71-1009); and Burnie (48 Cattley St., tel. 004/30-2224). Most of these offices are open from 8:45 a.m. to 5:45 p.m. weekdays, 9:00 to 11:00 a.m. Saturdays.

In Melbourne, Tasbureau is at 256 Collins St. (tel. 03/63-6351) and in Sydney, at 129 King St. (tel. 02/233-2500). In North America, write c/o the Australian Tourist Commission, Suite 1740, 3550 Wilshire Blvd., Los Angeles, CA 90010 (tel. 213/380-6060).

Two publications produced by Tasbureau are invaluable. *The Visitor's Guide to Tasmania* will tell you about every tourist attraction in the state. The bimonthly *Tasmanian Travelways* newspaper tells you how to get there, where to stay and where to eat, and how much it will cost you.

ADELAIDE AND SOUTH AUSTRALIA

South Australia calls itself the "WOW" state—wine, opals, and wildlife. The Barossa Valley northeast of Adelaide is Australia's premier wine-producing district; Coober Pedy, in the state's scorching outback, is the country's best-known opal-mining center; and Kangaroo Island, off the south coast, may have a richer concentration of native fauna than any other part of the nation.

Adelaide, the pleasant capital of South Australia, is a perfect staging point for reaching these and other outlying attractions. Though Adelaide, with few points of major tourist interest, may come across to visitors as "a big country town," its urban population of 900,000 is two-thirds that of the entire state. The city center is lovely, carefully platted beside the River Torrens and completely surrounded by a ring of spacious parkland.

I won't suggest a schedule here, since South Australia's attractions are in various directions from Adelaide and may not be

Greater Adelaide

TO PORT AUGUSTA, ALICE SPRINGS & PERTH

Hamley Bridge

Kapunda

TO RENMARK & SYDNEY

Nuriootpa

Tanunda

N

Two Wells

Gawler

Angaston

Lyndoch

ELIZABETH

St. Kilda

Mt. Pleasant

Outer Harbor

Birdwood

Tea Tree Gully

Port Adelaide

TO MANNUM

Lobethal

TO KANGAROO ISLAND

Grange Henley

ADELAIDE

Woodside

Glenelg

Brighton

Hahndorf

Reynella

Clarendon

Mount Barker

Christies Beach

GULF ST. VINCENT

McLaren Vale

TO MURRAY BRIDGE & MELBOURNE

Strathalbyn

Langhorne Creek

Mount Compass

Normanville

Goolwa

Victor Harbor

Cape Jervis

ENCOUNTER BAY

practical to include in one itinerary without considerable time and/or money. Pick and choose spots that pique your interest.

Getting There

The major domestic carriers, Ansett and Australian airlines, serve Adelaide with nonstop daily flights to and from Sydney, Melbourne, Perth, and Alice Springs and regularly scheduled direct flights to and from Brisbane, Canberra, Darwin, the Gold Coast, and Queensland's Sunshine Coast. Air time from Sydney is about 1 hour, 50 minutes; from Perth, it's about 3 hours. South Australian time is 30 minutes ahead of Sydney, Melbourne, and Brisbane, but 1½ hours behind Western Australia. Several small carriers service local routes; most notable is Kendall Airlines, which flies an Adelaide-Coober Pedy-Ayers Rock service every Saturday morning.

You can rent a vehicle and drive directly from Melbourne, 747 km (464 miles) via the Western and Dukes highways, or Sydney, 1,433 km (890 miles) via the Mid Western and Stuart highways. Brisbane is 2,056 km (1,277 miles) by the shortest route, Alice Springs is 1,697 km (1,054 miles), and if you're really adventurous, Perth is 2,720 km (1,690 miles) across the treacherous Nullarbor Plain. (Null arbor = "no vegetation.") Interstate buses travel these highways daily.

Rail service is also regular and efficient, with daily connections from Melbourne and Perth, six days a week from Sydney, and the famous "Ghan" weekly from Alice Springs.

Getting Around

You can rent a car at the airport or take the half-hourly Transit Regency coach into the city for A$2.40. Once you've arrived in Adelaide, the public transportation system—called the **State Transport Authority** (12A Grenfell St., tel. 210-1000)—will take good care of you. Buses run north to Elizabeth, south to Reynella, and east through the many communities of the Adelaide Hills. Suburban trains operate over a wider area, while the city's only electric tram links downtown with the seaside suburb of Glenelg. The interconnecting services run from 6:00 a.m. to 11:30 p.m. Monday to Saturday, 9:00 a.m. to 10:30 p.m. Sunday. Fares start at 70 cents. The **Adelaide Explorer Bus** (tel. 212-7344) stops at eight points on a 34-km (21-mile) circuit around the city; passengers who pay the A$6 adult fare can freely board and disembark over the course of the day.

Adelaide Highlights

It makes sense for Adelaide visitors to focus their sightseeing attentions on ▲▲ **North Terrace**, the broad thoroughfare that demarcates the north end of downtown. On or near this street, you'll find the Adelaide Casino, Constitutional Museum, the Festival Centre, Government House, State Library, South Australian Museum, Art Gallery of South Australia, University of Adelaide, Ayers House, and the Botanic Gardens—all within a five-block stretch.

▲▲**The Festival Centre**, on King William Road within a diva's trill of North Terrace, is Adelaide's best-known building and the site of a major international arts festival in February and March of every even-numbered year (i.e., 1988, 1990). This performing arts complex contains a concert hall, three indoor theaters, and an open-air amphitheater. Guided tours, A$2, are offered hourly on weekdays from 10:00 a.m. to 3:00 p.m. and four times Saturday between 10:30 a.m. and 3:00 p.m. Book with the tours office (tel. 216-8713).

▲▲**The South Australian Museum** is one of Australia's best museums, particularly for anthropology and geology. Of special note are the Aboriginal artifacts and Australite meteorites, both said to be the world's largest collections of their types. Open daily 10:00 a.m. to 5:00 p.m., except Wednesday from 1:00 p.m. and Sunday from 2:00 p.m. Admission is free.

▲**The Art Gallery of South Australia**, next door to the museum, has the requisite displays of Australian, English, and European paintings and decorative arts, plus a fine collection of Asian ceramics: Chinese, Annamese, and Thai. Open daily 10:00 a.m. to 5:00 p.m. Admission is free.

▲▲**The Migration and Settlement Museum**, behind the State Library at 82 Kintore Ave., recounts the struggle of Australian immigrants of the nineteenth and twentieth centuries and highlights the cultures of eight leading ethnic minorities of modern South Australia. Open 10:00 a.m. to 4:00 p.m. Monday to Saturday, from 2:00 p.m. Sunday. Admission is free.

▲**The Constitutional Museum** of political history occupies the former South Australian Legislative Council chambers, built in 1855. A walking tour costs A$1; if you've got a spare hour and 40 minutes, the audiovisual presentation "Bound for South Australia" relates a full social and political history of this state for A$3. Open weekdays 10:00 a.m. to 5:00 p.m., weekends 1:30 to 5:00 p.m., plus Wednesday nights 6:00 to 9:30 p.m.

▲**Ayers House**, 288 North Terrace, is a nineteenth-century mansion furnished in period style. Built in stages between 1846 and 1875, it was the residence of Sir Henry Ayers, premier of South Australia. Today, it contains two restaurants and the local headquarters of the National Trust. Open for inspection Tuesday to Friday 10:00 a.m. to 4:00 p.m., weekends and holidays 2:00 to 4:00 p.m. Guided tours, A$2, are offered by appointment (tel. 223-1655).

▲**The Zoological Gardens** on Frome Road have a superb collection of native birds plus many rare specimens bred in captivity. Open 9:30 a.m. to 5:00 p.m. daily. Admission is A$5.

▲**The South Australian Maritime Museum**, 119 Lipson St., Port Adelaide, has an enormous collection of marine artifacts documenting South Australia's maritime history.

▲**Glenelg** is Adelaide's most famous beach, a short trip from the city center by tram. Capt. John Windmarsh landed here and proclaimed the colony of South Australia in 1836; a replica of his boat, the HMS *Buffalo*, contains restaurants and a museum. Down the shore is a major amusement center, Magic Mountain.

▲**Carrick Hill**, 590 Fullarton Road, Springfield, a circa-1939 Elizabethan-style manor house surrounded by 96 acres of gardens and bushland, contains a priceless private art collection of nineteenth- and twentieth-century oils, silver, pewter, and furniture.

▲▲▲The **Adelaide Hills** rise above the coastal plain 20 minutes' drive east of the city center. Their charm is in their views, bushland reserves, and numerous unique villages scattered through the gentle valleys. **Hahndorf**, 28 km (17 miles) from Adelaide, was founded in 1839 by German refugees and is still "sehr Deutsch": many original stone buildings house hotels, restaurants, and artisans' studios. **Birdwood Mill National Motor Museum** at Birdwood has 300 vintage vehicles and other antiques in an old flour mill. **Cleland Conservation Park**, on the slopes of 2,333-foot Mount Lofty, is a great place for bushwalking and for viewing native wildlife.

South Australia Highlights

▲▲▲The **Barossa Valley** is the largest wine-producing district in Australia's major wine-producing state. Fifty separate wineries, most of them located in a stretch of 23 km (14 miles) along the Barossa Valley Highway between Lyndoch and Nuriootpa, open their cellar doors daily for tastings of their exquisite clarets and rieslings. The center of the region is Tanunda, a German town established in 1843 and the focus of the Barossa Valley Vintage Festival, held in April of every odd-numbered year (i.e., 1989, 1991).

▲▲The **Flinders Ranges** comprise a majestic set of sharp granite peaks and deep gorges 350 to 620 km (215 to 385 miles) north of Adelaide. Within this wilderness are ancient Aboriginal sites, abandoned mining towns, geological oddities, two national parks (Flinders Ranges and Gammon) and the Wilpena Pound, an enormous natural amphitheater surrounded by steep cliffs.

▲▲▲**Coober Pedy** is one of the world's most unusual communities. Most of the 2,100 residents of this opal-mining town, 943 km (586 miles) northwest of Adelaide by road, live in underground "dugouts" (homes) to escape the blistering desert heat. (The town's name derives from an Aboriginal phrase, "kupa piti," meaning "white man's hole.") More than half the world's opals are mined at Coober Pedy. You can see demonstrations of opal cutting and polishing, or even get a budget bed, at the Umoona Mine; explore an underground display home and church, visit a museum, and shop for raw or cut opals. Coober Pedy is a good overnight stop between Adelaide and Alice Springs. Its distinctive Desert Cave is billed as the world's first high-class underground hotel.

▲▲**Kangaroo Island**, Australia's third-largest offshore island, is best known for its plentiful wildlife. Some 150 km (90 miles) long, it is connected to Adelaide by four flights a day (A$84 return) and a daily ferry from Cape Jervis (A$22 one way, leaving at 10:00 a.m., arriving at 11:30 a.m.). If you want to make it a day trip, rent your car in Adelaide and drive onto the ferry (A$50 one way). The main town, Kingscote, is a farming center, but the main visitor draw is Flinders Chase National Park, where kangaroos, koalas, emus, and other native species run wild. Divers enjoy exploring offshore shipwrecks; fishing, bushwalking, and sunning on the beaches are also popular.

▲▲The **Murray River** is Australia's "Old Man River." Longer, at 1,609 miles, than most U.S. rivers (except the Mississippi, Yukon, and Missouri), it drains almost one-seventh of the Australian continent. Its final (and broadest) 400 miles cut through South Australia, emptying into Lake Alexandrina and Encounter Bay just south of Tailem Bend. You can cruise the river aboard a fully contained paddle wheeler like the *Proud Mary*, which sails between Murray Bridge and Renmark on 5-day or overnight cruises (33 Pirie St., Adelaide; tel. 08/51-9472); or rent your own houseboat: contact the Lower Murray Regional Tourist Association, P.O. Box 344, Murray Bridge, SA 5253 (tel. 085/32-6660), for booking details.

Helpful Hints

The **South Australian Government Travel Centre**, 18 King William St. near North Terrace (tel. 212-1644), operates a free information and booking service for hotels and tours throughout Adelaide and the state. It's open Monday to Friday 8:15 a.m. to 5:30 p.m., weekends and holidays 9:00 a.m. to 2:00 p.m.

PERTH AND WESTERN AUSTRALIA

Perth doesn't fit neatly into a 22-day itinerary merely because of its isolation from the rest of Australia. Adelaide, some 2,200 km (1,400 miles) distant (by air), is the nearest city with more than

25,000 people, and Jakarta, Indonesia, is closer to Perth than the Australian national capital, Canberra.

For those with time, however, it's well worth a visit. Perth, where 1 million of the 1.5 million Western Australians live, is a lovely Mediterranean-style city nestled along the shores of the broad Swan River. Best known in recent years as the temporary (1983-1987) home of the America's Cup of yachting, Perth is the gateway to a vast and varied state that is larger than France.

Suggested Schedule	
Day 1	Arrive in Perth. Enjoy a walking tour of the city, from London Court to Kings Park.
Day 2	Spend the day in Fremantle, an atmospheric European-style port town and the site of the 1987 America's Cup yacht races.
Day 3	Cruise the Swan River, passing the Royal Perth Yacht Club and continuing to Rottnest Island, where you can bicycle among the quokkas.
Day 4	Final sightseeing before an onward flight.

Getting There

Ansett and Australian airlines have nonstop daily flights to Perth from Adelaide, Melbourne, and Sydney and regular direct flights from Brisbane, Cairns, Mount Isa, Alice Springs, Darwin, and Port Hedland. Air time from Sydney is about 4½ hours, from Adelaide around 3 hours. (Perth time is 2 hours behind Sydney and Melbourne, 1½ behind Adelaide and the Northern Territory.) Think twice before driving across the seemingly endless Western Australian desert to Perth. Taking the train, however, is a wise alternative to flying. The "Indian-Pacific" takes 66 hours from Sydney, via Broken Hill, Adelaide, and Kalgoorlie, three times a week; the "Trans-Australian" runs 38 hours from Adelaide (with connections from Melbourne) twice a week.

Getting Around

Rent a car at the airport, 11 km (7 miles) from downtown, take the Skybus coach to downtown Perth or major hotels for A$5, or catch a city bus. The public transportation system, called **Transperth** (125 St. George's Terrace, tel. 221-1211) operates buses and trains weekly from 6:00 a.m. to 11:00 p.m., with reduced services on weekends and holidays. Tickets good for two hours on all services cost A$1; a day's pass is A$4. Free buses circle the city at 10-minute intervals from 7:30 a.m. to 5:30 p.m. weekdays, 9:00 to 11:30 a.m. Saturdays.

Metropolitan Perth

Perth Sightseeing Highlights

▲▲A walk down **St. George's Terrace** offers a look at some of Perth's most historic buildings, dating from the 1850s, plus some unusual shopping arcades—notably **London Court**, reminiscent of a quaint Elizabethan-era alley.

▲▲**Kings Park** overlooks the west side of downtown. This 1,000-acre expanse, one of Australia's nicest city parks, contains a botanical garden, a restaurant, numerous picnic grounds, fountains and memorials, and some grand views across Perth and the Swan River.

▲▲The **Western Australian Museum**, Francis at Beaufort Street, Northbridge (across the railroad tracks from downtown), is interesting for its natural antiquities—an 11-ton meteorite, for instance, and a 30-foot whale skeleton. It also has an Aboriginal gallery, wildlife displays, and the original 1856 Perth jail.

▲**The Art Gallery of Western Australia**, adjacent to the museum on James Street at Beaufort, shares the Perth Cultural Centre with the Alexander Library. The A$10 million gallery has a superb permanent collection of Australian (especially W.A.) and foreign works, among them Cezanne, Monet, Picasso, Rembrandt, Renoir, Van Gogh, and Whistler, plus a fine display of tribal art and regional crafts.

▲▲▲ **Swan River cruises** leave from the Barrack Street Jetty at the foot of downtown. **Transperth** offers a 2:00 p.m. upriver cruise daily (returning at 4:45 p.m.) with an adult fare of A$8; **Captain Cook Cruises** has three-hour daily cruises priced at A$12, leaving at 1:45 p.m. daily; **Golden Swan Cruises** offers full-day excursions to Fremantle for A$33, including lunch and sightseeing, or three-hour afternoon tea cruises for A$12. A fourth operator with trips to Fremantle and upriver to Swan Valley wineries is **Boat Torque Cruises**. Your narrator will point out the Royal Perth Yacht Club—the holder of the America's Cup from 1983 to 1987—and the homes of many of the city's wealthier residents. You'll also see a great many sailboards and other water sports. With no major industry on the river, it is virtually without pollution.

▲▲▲ **Beaches** in Perth are among the finest in Australia. Long strands of shimmering white sands extend from the Swan River mouth at North Fremantle for many miles north. Best known, from south to north, are **North Cottesloe**, Prince Charles' personal favorite; **Swanbourne**, Perth's No. 1 nude beach; **City Beach**, a family beach with modern facilities; and **Scarborough**, site of the new A$100 million Observation City resort hotel complex.

▲▲ **Armadale**, a Perth suburb about 24 km (15 miles) south of downtown, is the home of **Pioneer World**, a re-created working village of the late 1800s with various merchants and tradesmen, a police station, fire station, general store, schoolhouse, theater, and a stream for gold panning. Nearby, you can regress a few more centuries at the **Elizabethan Village**, which contains replicas of Shakespeare's birthplace and other famous English buildings, plus antique weapons, armor, tapestries, and furniture.

Fremantle Sightseeing Highlights

Western Australia's major port, settled in 1829, is situated at the mouth of the Swan River, just 19 km (12 miles) downstream from Perth. At once more historic and more cosmopolitan than its "big brother," it features many nineteenth-century European-style buildings (more than 150 classified by the National Trust), an active and highly visible artisans' community, and of course its harbor and yachting marina. Fremantle is 35 minutes by Transperth train from downtown Perth; the one-way fare is A55 cents.

▲▲**The Fremantle Museum and Arts Centre**, 1 Finnerty St. at Ord St., is housed in a handsome stone building constructed in 1860 as a convict lunatic asylum. There are exhibits on the colonial history of Fremantle, the Swan River, and the Western Australian coast, plus a fine display of local ceramics, sculpture, textiles, paintings, and prints.

▲▲**The Western Australian Maritime Museum**, Cliff Street, exhibits artifacts of W.A.'s rich trading and whaling history. Its star attraction is the *Batavia*, a Dutch sailing vessel shipwrecked in 1629 and now being reassembled timber by timber in the museum.

▲**The America's Cup Museum**, 43 Swan St., North Fremantle, has a collection of model yachts from the first America's Cup race through to the 1987 series, when the swiftest 12-meter sailing boats in the world made their homes in Fremantle for several months. The York Motor Museum of vintage cars is also at this address.

▲▲**The Round House**, on Arthur Head at the west end of High Street, is the state's oldest surviving building. Constructed in 1831 as the Swan River Colony's original civil jail, it affords an excellent view across Fremantle and the harbor. Other convict-era structures include the grim-looking **Fremantle Gaol**, The Terrace (off Fairbairn Street), built by convicts between 1851 and 1859 and still used as a prison, and the **Warder's Quarters** on Henderson Street, stone terrace houses for prison guards and wardens.

▲**Fremantle Markets**, South Terrace and Henderson Street, are a great place to browse for an artsy bargain or indulge in a variety of ethnic foods.

Rottnest Island

Perhaps the biggest surprise of many on this 5-by-11-km (3-by-7-mile) island, 18 km (11 miles) offshore from Fremantle, is that real estate developers haven't given it a new name. Its present monicker was provided by Dutch Commodore Willen de Vlamingh in 1696 when he mistook the native quokkas, miniature kangaroos, for rats. Developed in the 1830s as a convict farm colony, it was converted to minor resort status in 1917. The **Rottnest Museum,** housed in the 1857 grain-crushing mill, will tell you about the island's historic cottages and natural history. The **Underwater Explorer**, a semi-submersible submarine, offers cruises to look at shipwrecks, marine life, and reef formations. But the best way to see the island is to rent a bicycle from **Rottnest Bike Hire**, just behind the Hotel Rottnest, and pay A\$5 to pedal around for half a day. (There are no cars on the island.) Visit the salt lakes with their rich bird life, World War II gun emplacements, a lighthouse on the island's highest point, and impressive sandy beaches inviting you for a swim. You're almost sure to see the friendly little quokkas: the entire island is a wildlife sanctuary.

Get to Rottnest aboard the M/V *Temeraire II* from Barracks Street Jetty in Perth (A\$18 same-day return) or Fremantle (A\$14 return). It's about a 1½-hour ride from Perth. Boat Torque Cruises also operate daily package cruises, leaving Perth daily at 9:00 a.m. (returning at 5:45 p.m.) for A\$37 to A\$42, including lunch at Rottnest and a two-hour bus tour of the island. By air, its A\$19 return to Rottnest from the Perth Flight Centre at Perth airport, or A\$25 return on the *Island Hopper* helicopter from the Port Beach Road terminal in North Fremantle. Several lodgings are available on the island.

Highlights of Western Australia

Western Australia is Australia's largest state, sprawling across 965,000 square miles from the tropical Kimberley to the forests and meadows of the Southwest. Most of it is foreboding desert and stark terrain suitable for miners and kangaroos. But there are numerous areas of tourist interest for those with time and inclination.

▲▲The **Southwest** is the state's most fertile region. Besides its orchards, vineyards and cattle farms, there are surfing beaches and limestone caves along the west coast, forests of karri trees (300 feet high, 23 feet around) near Pemberton, the startling bluffs of the **Stirling Range National Park**, and the famous **Wave Rock** near Hyden. The largest towns are **Albany** (pop. 22,000), a beach town and agricultural center, and **Esperance** (pop. 7,000), gateway to the Archipelago of the Recherche, famous among divers. Australians flock to the Southwest in droves between August and November, when spring speckles the meadows and mountain slopes with 8,000 varieties of colorful wildflowers.

▲▲The **Goldfields** district focuses on **Kalgoorlie** (pop.

25,000), center of the state's gold-mining industry, 597 km (371 miles) east of Perth. Not quite a century ago, some 200,000 hopeful "diggers" worked this desert region seeking their fortunes. Kalgoorlie's wide streets and false-fronted hotels today are reminders of the gold rush era. Travelers visit the Hainault Tourist Mine to learn past and modern gold-mining methods, both under and above ground. Brothels, not legal, are tolerated here. Most of the nearby towns built in the decade following the 1893 discovery of gold—like Gwalia, Broad Arrow, and Menzies—are now ghost towns. Alone among them, **Coolgardie** has been preserved as a living monument to the era, although its population has shrunk from 15,000 to 900. Don't miss the **Goldfields Museum**, open daily.

▲▲The **Midlands** include numerous fascinating attractions within a day's drive north and east of Perth. **The Pinnacles**, calcified spires of an ancient forest 30,000 years old, are in Nambung National Park. **New Norcia** is a fragment of medieval Spain, complete with a Benedictine monastery and an astounding museum and art gallery. **York** is the historical (1840s) center of the agriculturally rich Avon Valley.

▲The **North Coast** starts at **Geraldton** (pop. 21,000), a farming and lobster-fishing center 423 km (263 miles) north of Perth. Many famous shipwrecks, including the 1629 *Batavia* disaster, occurred in the Abrolhos isles offshore. A short distance north is the self-proclaimed **Principality of Hutt**, where Prince Leonard, a former farmer with his tongue firmly in cheek, even issues his own postage stamps. **Kalbarri National Park** features some spectacular gorges on the Murchison River. **Carnarvon** (pop. 5,000), 801 km (498 miles) from Perth, is famous for its banana farms and prawning. **Port Hedland** (pop. 12,000), 1,547 km (978 miles) from Perth on Highway 1, is the principal port for the Pilbara, Australia's major iron ore region. At nearby Marble Bar, temperatures once exceeded 100 degrees F for five straight months.

▲▲The **Kimberley** is a remote, rugged region best seen during the cool, dry winter season (May to August). **Geikie Gorge**, on the Fitzroy River, and **Windjana Gorge**, on the Meda, are the most remarkable of several grandiose chasms in the King Leopold Ranges. **Tunnel Creek** has gouged a half-mile natural tunnel through limestone. The indented coastline is notable for its prolific crop of crocodiles! (Tourists beware: an American woman was gobbled alive in 1987.) **Broome** (pop. 4,000), 2,151 km (1,337 miles) from Perth, is a former pearl-diving center that has shifted its economic base to cultured pearls. Its blend of Europeans and third-generation Japanese, Malays, and other Asians is unique in Australia. Northeast of the Kimberley,

Kununurra (pop. 2,500), 3,140 km (1,951 miles) from Perth, was founded in 1960 as a base for the massive Ord River Irrigation Scheme. Water sports and cruises are popular on Lake Argyle, W.A.'s biggest inland body of water. The world's largest diamond mine opened in the Bungle Bungle range near here in 1985 after a major deposit was discovered.

Helpful Hints
The **Western Australian Tourism Commission** has its offices at 16 St. George's Terrace, Perth (tel. 220-1700). For everyday tourism information and bookings, visit the **Holiday W.A. Centre** at 772 Hay St. in Perth (322-2999) or 4 High St. in Fremantle (tel. 430-5555).

DARWIN AND THE "TOP END"

The main reason to go to Australia's "Top End"—the northern crown of the Northern Territory—is to visit Kakadu National Park. If you saw *Crocodile Dundee* and savored the fantastic wetland wilderness in which most of the Australian segment of the movie was filmed, you know just what Kakadu looks like. You even saw Jabiru ("Walkabout Creek"), Mick Dundee's "hometown," near which park headquarters are located.

Darwin, the gateway to Kakadu, is the hard-drinking capital of the Northern Territory. It has survived Japanese bombing in 1942 and a devastating cyclone in 1974 to become an interesting cosmopolitan city of 65,000.

Your schedule in the "Top End" should allow you a day in Darwin, as much time as you can make available in Kakadu, and possible side trips to Katherine Gorge and/or the Aboriginal communities on Bathurst or Melville islands. Keep in mind, though, that the oppressively humid wet season, from late November through March, is probably not a good time to visit.

Getting There
There are direct daily flights to Darwin from Adelaide, Brisbane, Melbourne, Perth, and Sydney aboard Ansett, Ansett W.A., or Australian airlines, and additional direct flights (not daily) from Cairns, Mount Isa, and Port Hedland. Air time from Alice Springs is 1 hour, 50 minutes; from Sydney, 4 hours; from Perth (with one stop), 4½ hours. Ansett N.T. offers nonstop flights several times a week to and from Katherine, Tennant Creek, and Gove/Nhulunbuy in the Northern Territory. There are also international connections to Indonesia and Singapore. There's no train service to Darwin, but you can travel overland by private car—a grueling effort, not recommended—or by express

"The Top End"

Milikapiti
MELVILLE IS.
Paru
• Pickertaramoor
Cobourg Peninsula Nat'l Park
• VAN DIEMEN GULF •
DARWIN
Oenpelli
Humpty Doo
• Fogg Dam
Wildlife Sanctuary
Jabiru
Kakadu
National
Park
Batchelor
Litchfield Park
Adelaide River
Waterfall Creek Nature Pk.
Daly River
Butterfly Gorge Nature Pk.
Pine Creek
Katherine Gorge National Park
KATHERINE
N
Mataranka

coach. No doubt the cheapest way to reach Darwin from major
population centers is with an unlimited-mileage bus pass from
Ansett Pioneer, Greyhound, or Deluxe Coaches. From Alice

Springs, buses normally take 21 hours (overnight) and charge A$107.

Getting Around

From Darwin airport, 6 km from town, you can rent a car, take an A$8 taxi ride, or hop on the airport shuttle bus for a A$2.50 ride into downtown. Within the city, public buses (tel. 81-2150) operate 6:00 a.m. to 11:00 p.m., Monday to Saturday, at a cost of A30 cents a ride. You can also rent bicycles for A$5 a day at **City Cycle Rental**, 69 Mitchell St. in the Greyhound depot.

You can take a long-distance coach to Katherine, but to Arnhem Land or the offshore Aboriginal reserves, you're best off to book a company tour, several of which are available.

Top End Sightseeing Highlights

▲▲**Darwin**, founded in 1869, was named after naturalist Charles Darwin by the captain of H.M.S. *Beagle*, who discovered the harbor 30 years earlier. The main sights include the **Botanical Gardens**, established in 1891 and now containing more than 400 species of tropical plants on 85 acres; **Doctor's Gully**, where thousands of ocean fish come in at high tide daily for a free feed of bread; the **Northern Territory Museum of Arts and Natural Sciences**, notable for its primitive art and wildlife exhibits; and the **Artillery Museum**, with reminders of Darwin's World War II buffeting. If you're up here in June, don't miss the annual **Beer Can Regatta**. Darwinites, who consume an average of 60 gallons of beer per year for every man, woman, and child, save up their empty cans for 51 weeks in order to construct an imaginative flotilla that sets sail on Darwin Harbour.

▲▲▲**Kakadu National Park** has been called the greatest wetland remaining on Planet Earth. Over 2,300 square miles in area, it comprises the floodplains of the East, South, and West Alligator rivers and the Wildman River, and the sudden cliffs of the Arnhem Land escarpment with gorges, waterfalls, and 18,000-year-old Aboriginal rock paintings. Join a safari for one to eight days of bushwalking, camping, and cruising the rivers. After joining one such expedition, my friend Elaine was ecstatic. "Talk about a once-in-a-lifetime experience!" she said. "I saw five crocodiles, water buffalos, kangaroos, dingos, bats and more birds and insects than you can imagine. The place was literally teeming with life." Book a trip from Darwin with **Terra Safari Tours**, 1585 Strath Road, Berrimah, NT (tel. 089/84-3470); **Australian Kakadu Tours**, P.O. Box 1397, Darwin (tel. 81-5144); or **Dial-a-Safari**, 14 Knucky St., Darwin (tel. 81-1244). Costs average around A$100 a day.

▲▲**Bathurst and Melville islands,** traditional homes of the isolated Tiwi Aboriginal tribes, are situated 80 km (50 miles) north of Darwin across the Clarence Strait. Tiwi pottery and woodcarvings, especially ceremonial grave poles, are unique. Contact **Tiwi Tours**, 27 Temira Crescent, Darwin (tel. 81-5144), to book a highly worthwhile half-day (A$125) or full-day (A$185) tour between March and October.

▲▲**Katherine Gorge National Park**, 31 km (19 miles) from Katherine (pop. 4,500) and 388 km (241 miles) southeast of Darwin, is best known for its boat trips between the sheer, 200-foot-high walls of the chasm. Two-hour cruises run four times daily the rest of the year, for about A$10 adult fare.

Helpful Hints
You'll find the helpful **Northern Territory Government Tourist Bureau** at 31 Smith Street Mall (tel. 81-6611), open 8:45 a.m. to 5:00 p.m. Monday to Friday and 9:00 a.m. to noon Saturday.

GREAT BARRIER REEF ISLANDS

If a visit to Green Island (Day 17) whets your appetite for more time in the tropical sun, you'll be pleased to know that there are hundreds of other islands off the coast of Queensland between the Gold Coast and Cape Melville, spread across 1,300 km (800 miles) of South Pacific Ocean. Nearly two dozen of them have established resort settlements.

Getting There
The main gateway towns are Bundaberg, Gladstone, Rockhampton, Mackay, Proserpine, Townsville, Cardwell, Tully, Cairns, and Cooktown, scattered up the coast north of Brisbane. All are connected by highway; all but Cooktown are linked via rail; all but Cardwell and Tully have domestic airports of their own. Once you've reached the gateway town, it's a relatively painless procedure to get to the island by boat (every resort has its own launch service from nearby mainland harbors) or small plane. Inquire locally for directions or check with the nearest Queensland Government Travel Centre.

The busiest gateway town is **Proserpine**, the takeoff point for the Whitsunday Islands. Located 1,165 km (724 miles) north of Brisbane and 650 km (404 miles) south of Cairns, it is served by nonstop flights from Brisbane, Townsville, and Mackay several times a week and by direct flights (with stops) from Sydney and Melbourne. Coaches connect Proserpine with Shute Harbour, 22 km (14 miles) east, from which launches run several times daily to the various resorts of the Whitsundays.

Great Barrier Reef

COOKTOWN

CORAL SEA

Green Island
Fitzroy Island
CAIRNS
ATHERTON

INNISFAIL

Dunk Island
Bedarra Island
Hinchinbrook Island
Orpheus Island
INGHAM
Palm Island

Magnetic Island

TOWNSVILLE

GREAT BARRIER REEF

FLINDERS HWY.
CHARTERS
TOWERS

GREGORY HWY.

PROSPERPINE

Hayman Is.
Whitsunday Islands
Lindeman Is.
Newry Is.
Brampton Is.

MacKAY

BRUCE HWY.

CLERMONT

CAPRICORN HWY.
EMERALD
ROCKHAMPTON
Great Keppel Island
Heron Island

GLADSTONE

Lady Elliot Is.

BUNDABERG
Fraser Island

QUEENSLAND

MARYBOROUGH

1 INCH = 125 MILES

Island Highlights

Every Barrier Reef island has something a little different to offer the visitor. Some are upscale, jet-set resorts, with all manner of sports facilities and nightlife. Others are limited to rustic cottages or youth hostel accommodations. You're bound to find something to match your desires and price range.

The following listing singles out major resort islands (except for those covered in our Cairns itinerary), starting in the south and moving north.

Lady Elliot Island is the southernmost coral cay on the reef. Visitors come to this tiny isle to enjoy the marine life with tank snorkel or on foot at low tide. Full-board lodging costs A$55 to A$75 in scattered cabins or safari tents. There's no launch service; charter aircraft from Bundaberg charge A$95 return.

Heron Island is famous worldwide for its outstanding scuba diving and snorkeling. Just 42 acres in area, this unspoiled cay is surrounded by over 9 square miles of coral reef. The Barrier Reef Divers Festival is held every November; the rest of the year, you can get excellent diving instruction and equipment. In addition to the reef life, you can see green sea turtles and migratory mutton birds nest here (the island is a national park) and lay their eggs in spring and summer. Launches leave Gladstone daily except Thursday at 8:00 a.m., arriving at Heron Island (a distance of 72 km, or 45 miles) 2½ hours later, for A$100 return. Or you can take a helicopter for A$217 return.

Great Keppel Island is as frantic as Heron and Lady Elliot are serene. The largest of 27 mostly undeveloped islands in the Keppel Group, 13 km (8 miles) east of Yeppoon, near Rockhampton, it is heavily geared toward singles in their 20s. At the main resort, activities are scheduled every minute of the day and night, from water sports to disco dancing (there's a resident rock band), tennis and golf to squash and cricket. The resort is owned by Australian Airlines, which offers weekly packages. To get to Great Keppel, take a coach from Rockhampton to Rosslyn Bay (near Yeppoon), then pay A$12 return for the hydrofoil. There are also several 25-minute flights daily from Rockhampton.

Brampton Island, 32 km (20 miles) north of Mackay, is a national park and wildlife sanctuary. The mountainous, 1,100-acre island is cloaked in tropical forest and surrounded by white sand beaches and coral reefs. It's great for bushwalking among semi-tame kangaroos and colorful lorikeets. At Brampton Island Resort, an Australian Airlines hotel, activities include all manner of water sports, tennis and golf, and a disco for nightlife. Launch service operates daily from Mackay at 9:00 a.m. The cruise takes an hour, and the cost is A$24 return. If you prefer to fly, Air Queensland makes the short hop from Mackay.

Newry Island, a hilly, wooded national park of just 110 acres, is one of the least known (and most untouristy) of all the isles off the Queensland coast. Koalas and echidnas are native to the island, a good place for walking and swimming. A small resort accommodates 25 guests; camping is also available. A launch service operates from Victor Creek, 56 km (35 miles) north of Mackay, at 11:00 a.m. every Wednesday, Saturday, and Sunday. It takes 15 minutes; the fare is A$10.

Lindeman Island is on the southern fringe of the Whitsunday Group, 74 islands discovered and named by Captain Cook in 1770. Lindeman was the first of the Barrier Reef resorts, established in 1929 and still a favorite for many Australian families. Walking trails climb the hills of this rocky, 2,000-acre isle. There are organized activities for kids of all ages. Launch fare from Shute Harbour is A$20 return; flights from Proserpine are A$60 return.

Hamilton Island is the luxurious, world-class resort center of the Whitsundays. The A$200 million hotel complex features five restaurants and a French bakery, seven bars (including one of the swim-up variety in Australia's largest freshwater pool), an indoor sports complex, a shopping center with four boutiques, a 200-acre fauna park, a 400-boat marina, sportfishing charters and scuba-diving instruction, and a "floating hotel," the Coral Cat, hovering above the reef. The 1,200-acre island is quite hilly, but there's enough flat ground for Queensland's only island airport where large jets can land. Ansett flies nonstop daily from Cairns and several times weekly from Brisbane, Sydney, and Melbourne. A 45-minute launch service runs twice daily (9:00 a.m. and 4:45 p.m.) from Shute Harbour for a return fare of A$25.

Long Island has two very different resort communities about 2 km apart. The Ansett-owned Whitsunday 100 Resort competes for the 18-to-35 singles clientele of Great Keppel Island with nonstop water sports by day, disco dancing by night. A$85 to $90 per person. Budget travelers, meanwhile, enjoy Palm Bay Resort, cook their own food (there's a small grocery), and enjoy bushwalking and snorkeling. Long Island is a lush national park 11 km (7 miles) long, no more than 1½ km wide, and everywhere mountainous. Launches run four times daily (9:00 a.m. to 4:45 p.m.) from Shute Harbour, 8 km (5 miles) northwest. The round-trip fare is A$16 to Palm Bay, A$20 to Whitsunday 100.

South Molle Island is a 1,000-acre island of steep bush-covered hills and coral-fringed bays in the heart of the Whitsunday Passage. A national park, it is crisscrossed by walking tracks and inhabited by brightly colored lorikeets. The medium-sized resort offers water sports, fishing, a gymnasium, golf, and tennis. It is served by restaurants, bars, and other facilities.

Launch service from Shute Harbour (daily at 9:00 a.m., 1:00 and 5:00 p.m.) costs A$20 return.

Daydream Island is tiny, just three-fourths of a mile long and barely 500 meters (547 yards) wide. Social life on this speck of paradise, clutched by white coral beaches and lazy coconut palms, focuses on the resort's huge lagoon-style swimming pool with its bar on a central island (no "dry" martinis here). There are the usual variety of water and other sports and a disco for night. The island is served twice daily (9:00 a.m. and 5:00 p.m.) by launch from Shute Harbour, 5 km (3 miles) distant, for A$15 return.

Hayman Island, one of the oldest of the reef resorts (it dates from the 1950s), was reincarnated in 1986 as a five-star resort after a A$100 million renovation by Ansett. It's a universally appealing island with 1,000 acres of rugged mountain scenery, a wide fringe of reef, palm-shaded beaches, and dozens of species of birds and butterflies. The Ansett International Hotel has five restaurants, a library, a lively entertainment center, and fine water sports facilities. If you aren't in the mood for a cruise boat from Shute Harbour (A$25 return), you can fly by helicopter from Proserpine or direct by Turbo Beaver from Airlie Beach (near Shute Harbour) or Townsville.

Magnetic Island is almost a suburb of Townsville. Just 13 km (8 miles) north of Queensland's third-largest city, it attracts hundreds or even thousands of day-trippers. But it's big enough—20 square miles—that the throngs are easily escaped. Another mountainous national park island, it has fine bushwalking, a fernery and an aquarium, bird and koala sanctuaries, two dozen sandy beaches, and a motor road linking several resort villages along the eastern shore. (The island even has its own bus service.) You can rent bicycles or mopeds at Picnic Bay, where the ferry arrives 8 to 12 times daily from Townsville (35 minutes, A$6 return). The island contains at least a half-dozen official and unofficial youth hostels, numerous holiday flats, and economy-priced hotels in Picnic Bay and Arcadia. Australian Airlines' Alma Dean Beach Resort midway up the east coast is a top resort.

Orpheus Island is one of the more secluded of the reef resorts, 80 km (50 miles) northwest of Townsville and 24 km (15 miles) east of Lucinda, near Ingham. Eleven km (7 miles) long, not quite a mile wide, and fringed with reef, the forested island—volcanic in origin—is a national park rich in birdlife and turtle nesting grounds. There's no regular launch service, but seaplanes or helicopters operate daily from Townsville for A$155 return.

Hinchinbrook Island is the world's largest island national park, a 144-square-mile Tahitian landscape of lush rain forest, mist-shrouded mountains (up to 3,400 feet high), spectacular waterfalls, rocky caves, sandy beaches (on the east coast), and rich wildlife. A narrow channel separates it from the mainland east of Cardwell, about halfway between Townsville and Cairns. Launches leave Cardwell daily except Monday at 9:00 a.m., with a fare of A$24 return.

Bedarra Island is a tiny and exclusive resort island. One mile long and a half-mile wide, four miles off the coast near Tully, it is densely forested and ringed by white sandy beaches. The new Bedarra Bay Resort consists of 24 elaborate guest bungalows set in a tropical garden along the ocean. There's no organized entertainment of any type—nothing but "intimate, casual and elegant" relaxation, as promoters put it. No one under 15 is allowed. Reach Bedarra aboard a daily launch service via Dunk Island from Clump Point, near Tully (A$18 return).

Dunk Island is another unspoiled gem with a remarkably rich fauna and flora. Lush jungle caresses the slopes of 900-foot Mount Koo-tal-oo, providing a home for some 150 species of birds, plus dozens of beetles and butterflies, lizards and snakes, bats and echidnas. The island is only 520 acres in size, but it somehow seems larger. The sophisticated over-30s set likes its Great Barrier Reef Hotel, which offers all the sports of other island resorts plus horseback riding, skeet shooting, and nature activities. Get there on a launch from Clump Point, 5 km (3 miles) west, for A$12 return; water taxi from South Mission Beach; or a flight with Australian Airlines (the resort owner) daily from Townsville and several times a week from Cairns.

Lizard Island is the northernmost of the Barrier Reef resort islands, 95 km (59 miles) northeast of Cooktown. Situated close to the magnificent outer reef, this lovely 4-square-mile island has great beaches, better snorkeling, and some of the world's finest big-game fishing within easy cast. Lizard Island Lodge is an exclusive resort overlooking a coral lagoon. Air Queensland flies to Lizard Island at least once a day from Cairns (A$96) or Cooktown (A$58).

Helpful Hints

Queensland Government Travel Centres are situated in three towns between Brisbane and Cairns: Rockhampton (119 East St., tel. 079/27-8611); Mackay (River Street, tel. 079/57-2292); and Townsville (303 Flinders Mall, tel. 077/71-3077). The QGTC's main office is at 196 Adelaide St., Brisbane, Qld. 4000 (tel. 07/31-2211). Most of the reef resorts have postal service and shops; many also have banking facilities and resident medical practitioners.

Yes, Australians do speak English—but it often seems to be a different English language than most Americans are used to hearing. For starters, the dialect is a bit odd, with the long "A" sounding more like an "I" and the "R," except at the beginning of a word, often dropped altogether. Once you begin to become accustomed to that, you find that there's a whole new vocabulary you never learned in school. The following list is an attempt to make your understanding a bit easier.

"Strine," by the way, was one foreigner's attempt to transliterate the word "Australian" as it is sometimes pronounced.

Abo Aboriginal (derogatory)

amber beer

arvo afternoon

back of beyond the outback

back of Bourke way out in the outback

banana bender native Queenslander

barbie barbecue

barrack cheer the team to victory

beet root red beet (always on hamburgers and in salads)

belt up shut up

bent drunk or stoned

bickie (or biscuit) cookie

bike promiscuous woman

billabong water hole in an intermittent river

billy tin pot used to boil water for tea

bitser mongrel dog ("bitsa this, bitsa that")

bitumen surfaced road

bloke guy

bloody a universal expletive

blowfly the Australian national pest

blue fight

bludger human parasite, lazy person

bo peep quick look

bonnet hood (of a vehicle)

bonzer wonderful

boomer very large; especially, a large kangaroo

Boong Aboriginal (very derogatory)

boot trunk (of vehicle)

bottle shop liquor store

bowser gas pump; also, tanker truck

brumby wild horse

Buckley's chance a snowball's chance in hell

buggered exhausted; also lewd meanings

Bullamakanka beyond the back of Bourke

bull dust fine, powdery dust on outback roads

bush anything outside a town or city

bushranger nineteenth-century outlaw

bushwalking hiking

chemist pharmacist

chock-a-block 100% full

chook chicken

cobber mate

come a gutser make a bad mistake

come the raw prawn be deceitful

coolabah a type of eucalyptus tree

corroboree Aboriginal festival

cracker biscuit

crook sick, broken, or no good

cuppa cup of tea (or coffee)

cut lunch sandwiches

daks trousers

damper unleavened bread (bush tucker)

didgeridoo Aboriginal musical instrument; it drones

digger originally a gold miner; later a soldier; now, often, any Australian

dinkie die fair dinkum

dinkum honest, genuine

do your block lose your temper

drongo born loser, ne'er-do-well

dunny outhouse

Enzed New Zealand

evo evening

fair dinkum the complete, honest truth

flake shark meat (used in fish and chips)

flaming another all-purpose expletive

flog sell, vend

footie Australian football

g'day universal greeting

galah rose-colored parrot; also, a fool

get off your bike become angry

gin female Aboriginal (derogatory)

give it a burl give it a try

give it the flick get rid of it

going troppo moving to the far north

goodonya "Good on you," "Way to go"

grazier livestock rancher with large holdings

greenies environmentalists

hang a Louie do a left turn

hang a Roscoe do a right turn

hard case enjoyable person to be around

have on accept a challenge; also, pull one's leg

hump root; also, to carry (as a swag)

jackeroo apprentice cowboy

jilleroo apprentice cowgirl

jumbuck sheep

kip bed

Kiwi New Zealander

knackered exhausted

Lamington a cake with coconut-chocolate icing

Larrikin rabble rouser, hoodlum

lob arrive

lollies candy

lolly water soda pop

mate close friend (not spouse)

matilda belongings carried in a swag

middy medium-sized glass of beer

milk bar corner grocery

Moreton Bay bug a small yabbie

mozzie mosquito

Never Never desert land, inhabited by Aboriginals

nick steal

no worries she'll be right

Ocker stereotypical Aussie loudmouth

offsider assistant

on the turps off the wagon

Oz Australia

packet envelope, usually containing paycheck

pavement sidewalk

pavlova traditional Aussie meringue dessert

penguin nun

perve scope out an attractive woman or man

peter cash register

pinch arrest

point the bone hex (an Aboriginal superstition)

poker machine slot machine

Pom Englishman

pony small glass of beer

postie mail delivery person

pot a Victorian middy

power point light socket

prang crash or dent

rage party

randy sexually excited (horny)

rapt enthralled

ripper great!

roo kangaroo

roos in his paddock bats in his belfry

root sexual intercourse; does not mean cheering for a team!

schooner large glass of beer

sea wasp jellyfish with highly potent venom

sealed paved (as in a road)

Seppo American (from rhyming slang: Yank = Septic Tank = Seppo)

shandy a beer-and-lemonade drink

sheila young woman; "broad"

she'll be right everything will be OK (also "she's jake," "she's sweet," "she'll be apples")

shoot through leave suddenly

shop assistant sales clerk

shout buy a round of drinks

silk shirt on a pig something wasted

silver beet spinach

silvertail member of high society

sly grogger after-hours drinking establishment

smoke-o tea break

snag sausage

sprog baby

spunky sexy-looking

station large farm or ranch in the outback

stickybeak busybody

stone 14 pounds (weight)

strewth! It's the truth!

strides trousers

swag small bundle of personal belongings

swagman hobo

Sydney or the bush all or nothing

ta Thanks

TAB "bettin' shop": Totalisator Agency Board

takeaway bar fast-food restaurant

Tazzie Tasmania

togs swimsuit

too right without question

track outback road

tram streetcar

trendy akin to yuppie

tube can of beer

tucker food

two-pot screamer person unable to hold his beer

uni (or varsity) university

up a gum tree in a dilemma

ute utility truck; pickup truck

Vegemite a strong-tasting brown-yeast sandwich spread, *very* Australian

walkabout traveling on foot for a long way without a specific destination

walloper policeman

wharfie longshoreman

whinge complain

witchety grubs sweet worms, cooked in sauce

wowser killjoy

yabber chatter

yabbie crawdad (small lobster)

yakka work

Yank American

INDEX

Other Books from John Muir Publications

Elderhostels: The Students' Choice, Mildred Hyman (65-28-9) 224 pp. $12.95

Europe 101: History & Art for the Traveler, Rick Steves and Gene Openshaw (28-78-8) 372 pp. $12.95

Europe Through the Back Door, Rick Steves (65-42-4) 432 pp. $16.95

Floating Vacations: River, Lake, and Ocean Adventures, Michael White (65-32-7) 256 pp. $17.95

Gypsying After 40: A Guide to Adventure and Self-Discovery, Bob Harris (28-71-0) 264 pp. $12.95

The Heart of Jerusalem, Arlynn Nellhaus (28-79-6) 312 pp. $12.95

Indian America: A Traveler's Companion, Eagle/Walking Turtle (65-29-7) 424 pp. $16.95

Mona Winks: Self-Guided Tours of Europe's Top Museums, Rick Steves (28-85-0) 450 pp. $14.95

The On and Off the Road Cookbook, Carl Franz (28-27-3) 272 pp. $8.50

The People's Guide to Mexico, Carl Franz (28-99-0) 608 pp. $15.95

The People's Guide to RV Camping in Mexico, Carl Franz with Steve Rogers (28-91-5) 256 pp. $13.95

Ranch Vacations: The Complete Guide to Guest and Resort, Fly-Fishing, and Cross-Country Skiing Ranches, Eugene Kilgore (65-30-0) 392 pp. $18.95

The Shopper's Guide to Mexico, Steve Rogers and Tina Rosa (28-90-7) 224 pp. $9.95

Ski Tech's Guide to Equipment, Skiwear, and Accessories, edited by Bill Tanler (65-45-9) 144 pp. $11.95

Ski Tech's Guide to Maintenance and Repair, edited by Bill Tanler (65-46-7) 144 pp. $11.95

Traveler's Guide to Asian Culture, Kevin Chambers (65-14-9) 224 pp. $13.95

Traveler's Guide to Healing Centers and Retreats in North America, Martine Rudee and Jonathan Blease (65-15-7) 240 pp. $11.95

Undiscovered Islands of the Caribbean, Burl Willes (28-80-X) 232 pp. $14.95

Automotive Repair Manuals
How to Keep Your VW Alive (65-12-2) 424 pp. $19.95
How to Keep Your Rabbit Alive (65-21-1) 420 pp. $19.95
How to Keep Your Subaru Alive (65-11-4) 480 pp. $19.95
How to Keep Your Toyota Pickup Alive (28-81-3) 392 pp. $19.95
How to Keep Your Datsun/Nissan Alive (28-65-6) 544 pp. $19.95

Other Automotive Books
The Greaseless Guide to Car Care Confidence: Take the Terror Out of Talking to Your Mechanic, Mary Jackson (65-19-X) 224 pp. $14.95

Off-Road Emergency Repair & Survival, James Ristow (65-26-2) 160 pp. $9.95

Road & Track's Used Car Classics, edited by Peter Bohr (28-69-9) 272 pp. $12.95

Address all orders and inquiries to:
John Muir Publications
P.O. Box 613
Santa Fe, NM 87504
(505) 982-4078
1-800-888-7504